Acknow

Loving thanks to my husband, part ... port, insights and encouragement. I wou ... f all, Oriya and Hila, my daughters, for constantly reminding me of what is really important in life. I am grateful for having you.

My heartfelt appreciation to Andrew, Liat, Elinor, Eliran and Rachel, who were involved in the process of making the idea for this book a reality. I am grateful to my extended family and friends who provided encouragement and help along the way.

I would also like to thank my colleagues and friends Louise, Gila, Annette and Shani for their valuable comments. My gratitude to Liz for helping with the preparation of the book for as long as I have been writing, and to Maria for providing the final touches. I have appreciated their suggestions and insights. I would like to thank Maria from Swan & Horn Publishing House for believing in the book's message and approach.

And huge thanks to Harville and Helen for the Imago gift they gave me and the world, and for their endorsement. I would also like to acknowledge Roz who gave the book its title, and Netanel who offered important advice.

Appreciation too, to Liz from Fitzjohns Primary School and Ruthie from Oliver's Montessori nursery who let me observe their inspiring work in class. It is a privilege and joy to watch you work and connect with children.

Last, but not least, I would like to thank my clients, who encouraged and pushed me to write. Working with parents – who have the willingness to show vulnerability, strength and openness to work on and improve the connection and relationship they have with their children – is a privilege for me. Thank you for your trust. The changes that parents in my parenting groups, lectures, and private sessions created in their families inspired me to write this book.

SMALL STEPS TO

GREAT PARENTING

The Essential Guide
For Busy Parents

By Dr Kalanit Ben-Ari Ph.D.

ISBN 978-1722336301

Published by Swan & Horn, Scotland

Email: info@swanandhorn.co.uk

British Library Cataloguing in Publication Data: A catalogue record for this book is available from the British Library

For full details of our Archiving Policy, contact info@swanandhorn.co.uk.

Publisher's Disclaimer: Every effort has been made to ensure the accuracy of information contained in this publication, however no guarantee can be given that all errors and omissions have been excluded. The Publisher and Author accept no responsibility for loss occasioned to any person acting or refraining from action as a result of the content of this book.

Production and editorial: Hannah Phillips and Bethany Howell.

Covers and graphic design: Maria Hampshire-Carter and Shani Ivgi Barber.

To Oriya and Hila

For your gift
of showing me
where I need to grow

Contents

Welcome into this book

There is a saying among therapists that 'we teach what we want to improve in ourselves'. This is probably why the focus of my own work as a therapist, primarily with couples, turned more to therapy with parents soon after having my first child. As my own children reached toddlerhood, I found myself providing more and more consultations, lectures and workshops for parents. I noticed when I taught a specific topic that I became more conscious of it, and this greatly improved my relationship with my own children. Whenever I faced a parenting challenge, I offered a workshop on it. I realised that 'parenting' is like a muscle, one we need to use, to stretch, to exercise and to challenge; if we are persistent and flex the parenting muscle, we will enjoy the results of this flexible and healthy way of living.

Small Steps to Great Parenting has grown out of many years of experience as a family therapist. I started out working with deprived children living in a hostel. After completing a PhD in psychology, I began to work with couples and families at my private clinic. More parents came to see me for a wide range of reasons, covering all kinds behavioural challenges, communication issues and emotional difficulties. By this stage, they had often been inundated with complicated, out-dated and frequently conflicting advice, bouncing unsuccessfully from tolerating their children's tantrums to implementing time-outs and star charts. Time after time, they told me that rather than these kinds of short-term gimmicks, they wanted simple, effective tips for handling day-to-day situations that would work over the long term – tips that would allow them to communicate more effectively with their children.

All the parents who come to see me want to be the best parents they can be. They feel there must be another way to deal with their challenges. I teach them how to listen to what happens in the family dynamic, and I will do the same for you through this book. Using simple techniques, you will learn how to create a relationship with your children you've always desired.

How this book came about

It all started after a workshop I gave on the topic of sibling relationships. I was contacted by Alex, a father of three. My ideas and approach made a lot of sense to him, and he asked me whether I would consider putting tips and short ideas about parenting in a newsletter for people like him, who found it difficult to find time to read and digest the lengthy parenting books that were available. This is how the idea for this book was born – a comprehensive and *quick* guide for busy parents. I know how hard it can be for time-pressured parents to find either the time or energy to read the books they want to, especially when they are facing more challenges than ever before – increasing academic pressure on their children, and battles over screen time are just two examples.

Most parenting books on the market focus on problems that need 'fixing', usually to do with functions – problems with sleeping, eating, behaviour or toilet training. Of course, many parents are on the lookout for a 'quick fix' – some magic solution – but unfortunately there is no such thing! The key ingredients for successful parenting are deeper than that. They include thoughtfulness, planning and strategy, and consideration of your own values. As Harville Hendrix, the founder of Imago Relationship Therapy, once said: 'You cannot fix a relationship, but you can transform it'. The content of *Small Steps* is broken down into easily digestible concepts, with chapters which focus on specific areas that parents find challenging. It offers practical and easy-to-use tips which they can implement every day. All the suggestions relate to small changes that can make a big difference. Using just one tip a day can foster a joyful connection between you and your children.

This book is not about telling you a single 'right' way to deal with behaviour issues (which is what many parents believe the case to be) but gives a range of ideas. My aim is to support you to expand your options. I will help you tap into your own creativity in your parenting, so that you can discover which options are right for you. While it's tempting to delve into a book that deals with one specific issue – usually the most pressing one for your child at that time – this approach does not allow meaningful changes to occur. This is because it isn't possible to separate children's specific behaviours from the wider family dynamic. We need to look always at the big picture rather than the symptom – the underlying problem.

A colleague of mine compared the situation to a bagel – a dough ring with a hole in the middle. We can choose to concentrate on the hole in the middle, which represents the problem, but of course there's nothing there! Instead we should focus on the ring of dough, which represents our relationships. By making this ring fuller and bigger, the hole in the middle gets smaller – without you working on it directly. The book you are now reading is about the dough, about the many ways in which you can foster a positive and healthy connection between you and your children that not only makes your days more joyful, but also decreases any challenging behaviours in the family dynamic.

Overview of the content

Part One lays the foundations for positive and connected relationships between parents and their children. These basic principles, at the heart of our conscious relationships with our children, are described in the Introduction, which clarifies the difference between 'good' and 'effective' parents and describes why parenting can be so challenging, especially when we focus on the *relationship* rather than specific problems or discipline. It also illustrates the power of positive interactions, parental attitude and the process of change.

The chapters in this section focus on expanding your parenting skills, and giving you a 'toolkit' to equip you for your positive parenting journey – a journey that's about exploring and trying things out. There are simple techniques for reacting in a positive and encouraging way to a variety of day-to-day situations with your children, often very simple reactions that build trust and strengthen connections, so helping to create a positive atmosphere in the home, whereby the big picture of your values and goals as a parent translate into simple, everyday, hands-on interactions.

You will learn about the power of your words in daily interactions with your children, and the change that positive words can bring when coupled with a positive set of approaches. The *Beauty of Belonging* emphasises the importance of a child's sense of belonging to their family; much of their behaviour involves acting out actions when this is not the case. Non-verbal communication is covered too – children's unconscious minds react strongly to non-symbolic connections, and if you get this right you will bring more calm to their world, and yours. The tips in *Kindness Goes a Long Way* take you back to your own 'core intentions' to be a kind parent and role model – and underline the fact that kindness is the fastest way to bring about change. The child's point of view is covered in Chapter 5. Understanding their perspective promotes a healthy and connected relationship, and viewing things 'from their side' will change the way you react to them, in line with your values and their emotional and cognitive state.

Some parents need help when it comes to encouraging conversation (rather than interrogation), to improve their communication skills, moving away from 'master' talk and towards listening, validating, empathising and being curious. This is *hugely* significant to the parent–child relationship and for teaching and modelling to children how to communicate with others.

Ways to build your children's inner confidence in their own judgement are described in the context of teaching children to trust their instincts, which empowers them to make the right decisions for themselves when you are not around – something we all want. We all think that giving praise is the key to achieving positive outcomes for our children, but there is a downside that many of us are oblivious to – it can have many negative consequences. Praise is good, but it must be *effective* praise in order to increase their confidence and abilities, rather than create insecurities and a sense of inadequacy.

I also address play. It's a tricky subject in today's academically pressured world, but playtime can be used to develop creativity, and confidence, and learning – both your children's and your own.

Part Two looks at turning challenges (an inevitable part of the parenting experience) into opportunities, to move from a 'reaction' mode to a 'conscious and intentional' mode. The core principles of 'awareness' parenting are applied, in the context of the baggage that we all bring to our own families. Our own family backgrounds are very much linked to what we experience as parents, but they offer an opportunity to strengthen the connection we have with our children. There are many more suggestions for handling day-to-day challenges in the family.

In *Parenting Vision for Challenging Times*, you will bring your own 'core values' into your awareness to face challenging times. *Self-Disclosure Time* is crucially important for helping you understand (and let go) of old parenting patterns from your own parents, and create a new 'system model' for connecting with your children. Valuable insights into the words that parents tend to use over and over again are covered in *The Echo of Your Words*; these often lead to power struggles rather than fostering connection.

You will probably be aware of the new buzz word 'transitioning'. This is at the core of Chapter 13, dealing with the child's perspective. It offers more practical solutions for changing the atmosphere and energy at home, or when simply moving from one activity to another. The role of routine is discussed in the next chapter, especially for problem areas – bed-time, screen-time, and the morning rush. These tips help to bring order to the busy household, and make more time for fun! Another tricky area is sibling relationships. You can actively sew the seeds for lifelong friendship between your children, and learn how to deal with conflicts between them. Setting boundaries in a calm, confident and healthy way is covered in *Parental Authority*, with a focus on getting the balance right. Boundaries that are too strict or too weak create more problems than they solve.

Last, but not least, I discuss the importance of *Parents as a Team* – possibly the most important aspect of parenting! You will be shown ways to work together as co-parents and learn how this affects your children.

How to read this book

It might seem obvious, but please read this book in sequence. From front to back. Later, you can dip into it or use the index to find something specific. The background information and practical tips build upon each other to grow your knowledge and understanding as you go through it.

My overarching aim is to show you how to create the kind of connection you have always wanted with your children. This kind of relationship sometimes feels a long way away from the daily reality, but if you read my suggestions each day and embrace them as your family grows, your learning will become the most natural way to parent. It will take lots of practice with your 'parenting muscle' to begin with, but will quickly become easier.

And it will be fun! And in the years to come, you will love the results.

PART ONE

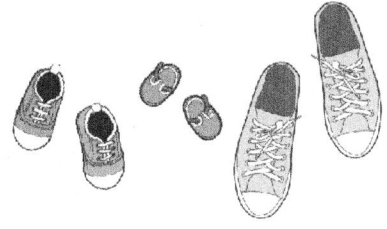

SMALL STEPS TO

Positive Parenting

EXPAND YOUR SKILLS

Introduction to Part One

A hundred years from now, it will not matter what my bank account was, the sort of house I lived in, or the kind of car I drove. But the world may be different because I was important in the life of a child.
Forest E. Witcraft

Good versus positive parenting: preparing for life

Are you a *good* parent? Yes, you are. You are reading this book and that speaks volumes! You love your children and you sacrifice your time, energy and money to give them everything they need. But the real question is: Are you an effective parent? Being an effective parent means that you invest your time and energy to reach a parenting goal, which is a long-term, meaningful goal. What is your parenting goal?

An effective parent realises that his or her job is to prepare a child for life, not by thinking that life can be made 'perfect' for them, but with the understanding that a confident, independent child with a sense of self-worth, efficacy and belonging will grow up to be an adult who can cope effectively with whatever life brings. In this respect, home is the practice ground for life. It is easier to learn and practice everything at home, and children can practice interpersonal relationships within a warm and protective environment.

Here's one example of the difference between 'good' and 'effective' parents. A parent who sleeps alongside his seven-year-old daughter, to help her get to sleep, is a good parent, giving time and energy and sacrificing his own needs, such as spending time with a partner or winding down for the evening. However, an effective parent will teach her to fall asleep by herself, thereby teaching her how to self-regulate her feelings in a competent and healthy way. It is this feeling of competence that creates a sense of capability which will accompany her over the years, throughout her schooling and into adulthood.

So, if your parenting goal is to prepare your child in a healthy way for life as a good and decent and capable adult, then consider how your actions today may bring you closer to this goal. This concept is at the very core of this book.

Focus on the relationship versus discipline

Most parenting books focus on the negative aspects of children and how to make them behave, how to cope with challenges in their eating and sleeping, how to deal with tantrums and toilet training, and so on. But as I pointed out before, focusing on the *negative* in this way will not yield the results you want

– neither in the short term nor the long term. Throughout my experiences as a mother, family therapist and researcher, I have learned that the focus should be on the *positive*. This allows parents to *empower* their children, by tapping into their own and their children's strengths, in order to deal with any challenges. When you use 'positive parenting' during your everyday interactions with your children, they learn more from you than you can imagine.

React positively in daily interactions

Why is it important to react in a positive way to your children during your daily interactions? To start with, it is the fastest way to motivate them to cooperate with the endless tasks of the daily routine. Children like to cooperate. They actually love to take part (believe it or not!) and they want to make you proud. In an emotionally warm and positive environment, they will thrive.

The first thing to understand is that reacting positively doesn't mean never saying 'No'. It doesn't mean that you need to serve your children's needs and wants all the time. What it does mean is that reacting in an assertive, conscious, thoughtful way – with respect for the child – brings kindness, warmth and positive energy to the relationship. Reacting positively creates a positive environment – and this simply makes a home a nice place to live.

When the atmosphere in the home is one of constant threats (*If you don't do it, I will...*) and peppered with punishments, raised voices and time-outs, or if it's one in which you constantly do for them what they can do (and should be doing) for themselves, then you may achieve good behaviour – for a time (this outcome is debatable, as I explain later). But don't mislead yourself into thinking that you have assimilated your values or that you are enriching your relationship with your child.

The alternative approach, using positive parenting techniques, not only serves your short-term goals of achieving cooperation, to create a relaxed atmosphere in the home and let you enjoy being with your children, but also strengthens your parent–child relationships. It teaches children something of your own values and increases their capabilities in the long term. A positive attitude will give you much more than a focus on discipline can offer.

Imagine the home you want to create

Imagine a scenario in which you have to choose between two families who have invited you to be their guest for a long weekend. You know nothing about either family, but you are allowed to peep through their windows and observe them for some time before you decide. You can't hear them – only watch their body language. Through the lounge window of the first house, you see a mother and a boy of about seven. You notice that the mother's body language is rigid and tense and she is pointing a finger at the boy. You guess that he's done something to upset her. He doesn't seem to be particularly bothered by this reaction, and continues to play on the iPad in his hands. Then a girl comes down the stairs, a little older than him, and sits beside him on the sofa. The mother is doing something in the kitchen, although it's difficult to see exactly what, and it is clear from her body language that she is not happy.

Now you look through the window of the second house. A young boy of a similar age is setting a table for dinner. The father is doing something in the kitchen, and again you can't see what it is, but you can see him looking at the boy from time to time with a warm smile. The older sister comes down the stairs, looking relaxed. The parent says something to her and she starts to help her brother with the table setting, chatting away as they work. Then they take out a pack of cards and start to play a game.

Which house would you like to stay in for the weekend? Although you couldn't hear anything, you can tell how the children are probably feeling in each house, and you can guess in which one they are more likely to feel empowered – which is what we all want for our children. Is your family more like the one in house one or house two?

The impact of positive daily interactions

Some parents I meet are initially sceptical about the difference that positive daily interactions can make to their children's lives. In practice, they find the benefits are many-fold. I have outlined just a few here.

BRAIN CHEMISTRY

Daniel Siegel, a *New York Times* bestselling author, neuropsychiatrist and inter-personal neurobiologist, explains in his book *Parenting From The Inside Out* that non-verbal communication, such as tone of voice, body posture and smile, can affect the physical development of a child's brain. This in turn can have a lifelong impact on his or her ability to relate to other people. It is astounding that simply by reacting in positive ways you can influence your child's brain! Of course, you influence the brain also when reacting in negative ways, which is what you want to avoid.

MODELLING

When parents invest in positive interactions, their children learn about themselves and about how to connect and relate to others, to communicate, to deal with success and challenges and to be with themselves and others. Parents are the most important role models for any child, especially because they learn from *actions* – not words. The findings of a recent study by Redding and his colleagues in 2016 revealed that parents who implement positive parenting techniques that they had learned on a course, experience more warmth towards their children and self-efficacy, and less hostility and stress.

INNER VOICE

Peggy Omara, the author of various parenting books and articles said: '*the way we talk to our children becomes their inner voice*'. In your everyday interactions with your children, you have the opportunity to grow their positive inner voice. You can build lifelong skills such as responsibility, curiosity, compassion, kindness, empathy and inner motivation by responding in a positive manner.

Make the 'in-between' moments matter

Do you remember what sort of home you used to return to from school when you were a child? Was it a smiley, warm, relaxed place? Or a grumpy, lonely, stressed one? Can you recall moments in which you felt joy and happiness? Exactly what kind of good things do you remember?

When I began asking parents on my courses these questions, it amazed me that it wasn't the big events they remembered most. It was the everyday ones: *When I went to the market with dad … When I helped mum with the cooking … When dad stroked my hair before I went to sleep … When I rode my bicycle with my brother.* Other parents remember things that might seem quite mundane: *When we watched the TV together and I felt my mum was enjoying it with me … When we walked in the park … When my dad read me stories.*

The truth is it isn't about birthday parties, trips abroad or shiny new computers, but the small moments – the moments in-between – that count. Moments where the child felt their parent was present in a warm way. These are the moments that fill our lives, day in and day out. In these moments, the magic happens.

Some people argue that nowadays things are different, with this so-called 'screen generation' that jumps from the iPad to the iPhone to the laptop, and these screens satisfy their wants and needs. I strongly disagree about this. I can promise you something: when you ask your child the above questions about their good memories in thirty years time, you will see that nothing has changed. They, as we do, will appreciate and be touched by the times their parents were present, connected and warm, and able to 'hold them in their mind'.

If your childhood home environment was warm and positive, you will probably find it easier to react in positive ways to your own children. But if you experienced stress, or grew up in a negative atmosphere, it might require more awareness and work for you to communicate positively. In either case, you cannot change your history, but you can create a positive and enriching environment for your children today. You can decide how to raise your children and which moments to create for them to remember.

"Mindful" versus "perfect" parenting

It can be overwhelming to know that in every interaction with your child you have the power to either wound their inner voice or to nurture a positive self-image. No-one expects parents to be positive *all* the time – it really isn't possible. Even if there were such a parent, I'm not sure the situation would be beneficial for the children. Some children's frustrations can be regarded as healthy, and *necessary* for them to learn how to cope in a healthy way with life's challenges. What I would like you to consider is about being *mindful* in the way you usually communicate at home.

Your behaviour is the mirror of your habits, and we all know habits are hard to change, but once you decide that you want to grow (and I say grow, rather than change, to acknowledge that we are all on a journey of development), then you can start using the simple tips in the next chapters. They are very easy and you will be surprised to learn that such small changes in the way you react make a huge difference to your parenting experience.

Live the change – and reap the rewards

I often hear parents say (following a workshop or session) that the first step for them was hearing themselves when they said something negative to their children. Afterwards, they became aware of their reactions and the effect they have on their children. Then they decided to practise and learn how to connect in a positive way. After some time, when reading over the notes they made during an early lecture or workshop, they can't believe they needed to write such things down, because the way they have come to think and act have become a natural part of who they are as parents.

In *Part Two* of the book, you will learn how to turn your challenges into opportunities. I will focus on how to react in positive ways to situations of conflict with your children, to help reduce your (and their) frustration and difficult behaviour. Recent research in this area (Bor *et al.*, 2002) reveals that facing conflicts with the foundation of positive and healthy day-to-day relationships reduces negative child behaviours such as aggression, extreme tantrums and opposition. Thus conflict is likely to become less frequent and less intense, turning instead into something that can be worked through, in which you can contain your children's feelings in order for them to be made sense of. While acknowledging that every child has their moments, a positive base will empower you to deal with them in a healthy way. So let's put our actions where our heart is and commit to positive parenting techniques.

- 1 -

Positive words create positive realities

Talking doesn't mean you have said something. What really matters is the message your words carry, not the sound, but the reverberation it causes on the soul.
Michael Bassey Johnson

Here we focus on ways you can use positive language in everyday interactions to create a positive atmosphere at home. Try using one a day if you can.

Reinforce the positive to address the negative

Parenting is a very creative job! We need to look for the positive even in the most challenging situations. I find that when I use positive language, I create a positive result. For example, when we were waiting at the doctor's to see a GP, I noticed that my young daughter started to lose patience after fifteen minutes. She started moving in her chair, up and down, becoming more and more restless. I picked up on what I saw and said:

'I really appreciate your patience. You have a lot of patience to wait so nicely. Do you want us to play something until we get called in?'

What do you think happened then? My daughter was more patient. What we notice and express in an empowering way is what grows. Children can recognise these qualities in themselves, and this is what builds their positive self-image. A parent once told me that her son was allowed to watch one programme on TV straight after school, but wouldn't always agree to turn the TV off afterwards. After hearing about my technique in a workshop, she responded to her son's request to watch TV by saying:

'Yes, you can watch your programme. I am really proud that last week you turned the TV off at the end of it.'

And the result? He turned it off by himself, and then he came to tell her that he had done it. So if you find yourself commenting again and again about your child's negative behaviour, why not try looking at it in a different way?

Be creative by seeing the positive and reacting to that.

"No, no, no!"

Whether we acknowledge it or not, most of our communication with our children involves asking them *not* to do things. This reminds me of *The Mom Song* by the American comedian Anita Renfroe, which was widely circulated on *YouTube*. She's a mother with three children who condensed what she typically says to her children in twenty-four hours into a song lasting two minutes and fifty-five seconds – much of it saying 'No' to what all children love doing the most: *Don't make a mess ... Don't play with the glue ... Don't put that in your mouth ... Don't play ball games in the house ... Don't jump ... Don't eat with your fingers.*

Yes, it is important for children to hear 'No' from time to time, but when it is the main word they hear at home, it won't contribute to the attitude that you would like your children to have. When we hear 'No, No, No' we start to react negatively. We no longer respond to the issues any more, but to the constant limitations. So what is the alternative?

First, be selective with your use of the word 'No'. Understand that children can and should be children and that this comes with mess, running, jumping and the other things they do.

Second, communicate some of the 'No's in a constructive way. At the end of the day, you want them to cooperate with you – not to create a power struggle. Here are a few examples:

> Child: 'Mum, can we play?'
> Parent: 'No, you should be ready for school by now!'
> *Replace this with:* 'After we've dressed, brushed our teeth and eaten, we can play.'

> Child: 'Dad, can I watch television?'
> Parent: 'No, we're eating.'
> *Replace this with*: 'Yes. Once we've all finished eating and cleared the table you can.'

> Child: 'Mum, can we play with this puzzle?'
> Parent: 'No. Look at all of the Monopoly cards on the floor!'
> *Replace this with*: 'Yes. You've already put the Monopoly board inside the box. All you have to do is to put all the cards in too. Then we can play with the puzzle.'

Can you see how the alternative works on the motivation to cooperate? It doesn't mean we do not say 'No' from time to time. It just means it's not the only word we are saying!

Stigma creates identity

Your words create your children's reality. For example, saying to a child 'You are not responsible' several times a day creates a child (and a future adult) who is not responsible. When you comment on your child's personality (You aren't kind ... patient ... responsible), they perceive it as a part of their *identity*. It becomes their 'stigma'. Stigmatising like this isn't productive. It is wounding and hurtful, and it kills motivation to change. When we tell our children *what* they are, it's very challenging for them to grow from that. In their head, they say: If mum says I'm not responsible, then who am I to contradict it? And what can we say instead?

Let's say your son stands with you before crossing the road and you notice that he puts one leg on the road, as if thinking to cross without checking whether it's safe. Rather than saying 'You're so irresponsible. You mustn't cross the road without checking', you might comment on his behaviour, and then add what you expect from him in that situation. Describe what you would like to see, not what you do not want to see. The result will sound something like:

'Crossing the road without looking carefully both ways is irresponsible behaviour. What do you think is sensible to do before crossing the road?'

'Before crossing the road, we need to look both ways and listen carefully for the sound of cars and motorbikes. Only when it's all clear is it safe to cross'.

This way the child can learn, and grow to *act* in a more responsible way. Now they will have the motivation to change their behaviour the next time they cross the road, or slice the bread, or pour the milk.

The test of time

Have you noticed that every time you hurry your children, they tend to slow down? So instead of rushing them, try giving them actual time limits, and communicate your expectations and their responsibility to be ready on time. This should, of course, be age-appropriate. Here are some examples:

'We're leaving for school at eight-thirty. It's eight-fifteen now.'

'The birthday party starts at two o'clock and it's one-thirty now.'

'As soon as you finish your homework, you can go to your friend's.'

'We're having dinner at 6 o'clock, when this hand reaches the number 12. Now it is ten to six so you have ten minutes to play.'

Awakening cooperation

If you are like many of the parents who attend my workshops, you will recall with frustration the times when you asked your children to do something and they were off in their own world, not hearing your request even though you asked them five times within five minutes. Their child might be playing by themselves, or daydreaming, or watching TV, so I give this tip in every Positive Parenting lecture I facilitate. The parents' reactions are always quite similar – they don't believe it can be so easy! I challenge them to try it and share their results. The day after the lecture, I inevitably receive emails saying 'It really works!'.

Think of it like this: when a child is in his or her own world, it is the same as when you are in a deep sleep (and we all know hard it is to wake up from a deep sleep). So the next time you find yourself in this situation, just ask – in a gentle voice (no shouting!):

'Lily, can you hear (mummy's/daddy's) voice?'

Children usually nod their heads, but if they don't, say it one more time. Then, in the same gentle and confident tone of voice, make your short request, and end it with a 'Thank you'. The 'Thank you' encourages the child to fulfil the request and at the same time gives the message you are confident that they will do it. In other words, you 'wake them up' gently before asking something of them.

Wean off "Why?"

Why? ... Why did you hit him? ... Why are you crying? ... Why do you look grumpy? ... I would like to encourage you to wean yourself off the 'Why?' questions. Sometimes children feel what they feel without knowing why – exactly like you do! So when we ask 'Why are you crying?' the child often cries more! Sometimes the 'Why' is not important – as in the case of hitting.

If there is a 'good' reason for the child to be angry, should they be hitting out? The 'why' isn't relevant. So replace it by mirroring your child's feeling, and help them to express that feeling in a more appropriate way. Here are some examples:

'I can see that you're very angry. Use words to explain what you're angry about – not your hands. Tell me "Mummy, I'm very angry. I want to go for a sleepover but you won't let me!" '

'I see that you're sad. Is it because Grandma left? Do you want a hug?'

'You look upset. Let me know if you want to talk about it'.

Preparing a plan

'What are your plans for the day?' This is a great question to start asking your children on a regular basis. Of course, they don't control all the day's activities, but they do have their own intentions.

This question encourages them to think about the day ahead and make their own plans – independence and taking responsibility for one's day starts here.

You can also use this question when they share with you some challenge they are having.

As British prize-winning science writer and author Roger Lewin says: 'Too often we give children answers to remember rather than problems to solve'. You can begin by asking your children:

'What do you think you should/can do about it?'

Choked by choice

Do you find it challenging when your children want to do things their way, but find it very frustrating to decide what their way is? For some children, it might be choosing what to wear; for others, what to play with; still others will want only one kind of food (pasta, of course), or prefer to skip out on a hygiene task like brushing their teeth.

With toddlers in particular, always be aware that asking open questions like 'What do you want to wear/eat/play?' and letting them choose can be an overwhelming and confusing proposition. Even for adults, making choices can be challenging – remember how you felt the last time you tried to choose between numerous brands of laptops in a shop.

The message is: keep it simple. You can do this, and help your child, by providing only two options to choose from. For example:

'Do you want the green or blue trousers today?'

'Do you want scrambled eggs or an omelette for breakfast?'

'Do you want to brush your teeth before or after getting dressed?'

Simple choices like this fulfil your child's *need* to have a sense of control – and yours to stay sane!

The wonder of words

When you become aware of the power of your words, then you become aware of how significantly you can connect with and strengthen your children. Your *words* become their *realities*. If you use *positive* words, you create *positive* realities.

Communicating in a negative way is a common pitfall for parents, but the following examples will illustrate my point.

A mother with a nine-month-old son came to see me. During the meeting, she changed his clothing. He was smiling and looked relaxed and happy. However, because she knew he liked to be naked (which she found frustrating), she said to him 'Oh, you're not going to try and take that off now, are you?'. And to me, she said 'He always does that'. As soon as she said that, he tried to get out of his clothes!

On another occasion, I heard a father telling his three-year-old daughter that she was too young to tie her shoelaces by herself and that he would need to help her. Unsurprisingly, she didn't even attempt the task.

Another time, I was eating out with another parent who said, in front of her child: 'She doesn't like to try new food and she never eats broccoli!', at which point the child refused the vegetables that were offered.

What's the alternative?

Well, you can begin by eliminating negative words like 'never' and reducing your use of the word 'no'. Better than that, you can try to anticipate positive outcomes, rather than negative ones. With regards to these above examples, the parents could have said:

> 'You look so lovely in this outfit' (Or she could have just smiled back at her happy baby.)
>
> 'Tying your shoelaces is tricky. I'm happy that you want to try. Let me know if you need help.'
>
> 'Would you like to try broccoli? What's the texture like? And the taste? Do you like it?'

It's useful to remember that if on a specific day, or in a specific week, your child doesn't want to eat or taste something, that doesn't mean they won't try it or like it in the future. Tomorrow is a new day and the child might *love* it tomorrow, because children are designed to grow and develop.

Every day is a chance to learn something new, experience something exciting, and grow in their abilities. Do give them the chance to surprise you! And start by being aware of the power of your words.

Left with the "but"

'You were really happy at the party, but you didn't behave ... The teacher said you're a caring friend, but you find it hard to concentrate in class ... You cleared up after yourself but you left glue all over the place!' These quotes illustrate the 'but' trick. You start off positive and then add a 'but'. Try to recall how this feels from the other side, for example, when your boss gave you positive feedback and then added a 'but' and followed it with a critique. Or when your partner said 'What great sex we had tonight – but why didn't you wear that outfit I like?' What are you left with? The 'but'. All the things before it just go blank, and it's the same for your child. What are the options here? Here are a few:

'You were really happy at the party. I expect you to express your excitement in a way that doesn't hurt others.'

'The teacher said you're a good friend – responsible and caring. She would like you to work on your concentration in class, too.'

'You cleared the papers, paint and leftovers. All that's left to do now is to clean the glue from the table.'

Help when needed

Despite liking to volunteer, there are those times when children can be over-tired, or feel unwell, or be overwhelmed by the task at hand. You might ask them to tidy up a game they've been playing with, to clear the table, or bring their night-clothes into the bathroom and not get the result you hoped for. Like in the example above, you can avoid using language such as 'should' and 'must,' and offer instead to be there to help if your help is needed. In line with many of the tips in this book, this puts the parent and the child on the same side – *against the problem* – rather than setting up a battle. For example, I recently observed this mother and child interaction:

Parent: 'Do you want to put the book back on the shelf?' *The child, after a day at the nursery, put it back in a messy way.*

Parent: 'Lets try nicely'—coming closer to the child and helping put back some other books. The child didn't succeed.

Parent: 'Try again' in a soft voice, and at the same time organized the other books on the shelf. The child succeeded.

Parent: 'That's it! Give me high five!'

The mother used positive words while still being assertive about the task. This, coupled with her body language and a calm tone of voice, communicated that she was there to help.

13

Who wants to volunteer?

We want to give our children more responsibility and we want them to cooperate with things like household tasks. But some parents very quickly turn simple 'helping' activities into unnecessary power struggles – often using words like 'you should' and 'you must'.

In truth, there are far more effective ways to gain their cooperation. As a parent, it's useful to recognise that for both children and adults, a sense of autonomy is an important component of their motivation to cooperate.

Children are dependent on adults on very many levels, but at the same time they (like us) do not like to be controlled. They like to believe that what they are doing is their choice, rather than an obligation, and they appreciate choice.

One of the ways I encourage my children to cooperate is by asking them, 'Who wants to volunteer?' For example:

'Who wants to volunteer to prepare the table for dinner?'

'Who wants to volunteer to put the clean clothes away?'

This places me and my children on the same side – namely, against the *task at hand* – and most of the time one of them comes to help. In the rare event that my question is ignored, I go to where they are, make eye contact with them and, in a kind voice, say:

'We have lots to do for dinner. When mummy asks who is volunteering I expect one of you or both to come and help. So now that I have asked, I'll be in the kitchen waiting for the volunteer'.

They both come.

- 2 -

The beauty of belonging

You're imperfect and you're wired for struggle,
but you are worthy of love and belonging.
Brene Brown

A sense of belonging is crucial for healthy development. This chapter provides tips that address ways in which you can develop it in your children, by reacting in a positive, encouraging way in your daily life.

Belonging as base

A sense of belonging means that we have a place and value in the world as we are. This is the feeling that we are loved and wanted, as well as being capable and contributing. It is a base from which to enjoy life's adventures. The result of a healthy sense of belonging is confidence, positive self-image, courage and optimism. A child who believes in themselves will want to contribute, learn and grow.

Without a sense of belonging, a child will feel rejected, incapable, not good enough, devalued, unnecessary and disadvantaged, and lack courage. This child will look for excuses and may seek value through negative behaviours.

In the Adlerian (psychodynamic) approach to parenting, many children's challenging behaviours are put down to their *lack* of a sense of belonging in their family, and they may behave negatively when their sense of belonging is questioned, for example, when they feel forgotten in the presence of a newly arrived sibling.

Although you might feel that your child is receiving enough attention, what is important is *how the child feels* because they might experience the family dynamic differently. They will react to their own subjective experience and, in doing so, their reality becomes their truth.

If you manage to cross the bridge to your child's world (or imagine your way into it), how much of a sense of belonging do you think they would feel?

Sharing is caring

With whom do we share our thoughts and feelings? With people whose opinions we value – people who are close to us. Sharing with your child (age-appropriately, of course) gets the message over that we value their opinion and feel close to them. Sharing creates intimacy and respect, and develops empathy and interest. It also models a way to communicate.

In the past, children grew up in communities, with extended family all around them, and without the modern technology of phones and computers to hand, people actually communicated! They did this face-to-face. They helped each other, and reached for solutions. And where were the children? Watching. Learning. Observing. Imitating. There was a *strong* sense of belonging in this context. They learned from their parents, their grandparents and their extended family, as well as the grocer and the milkman. They had endless opportunities to observe adults talking to other people and they learned what was helpful, useful, productive, interesting – and how to manage differences and create intimacy.

Nowadays, children are not exposed to this level of face-to-face communication. They do not read the texts messages you send to your partner or parents; they are not privy to the emails or Facebook interactions that you share with your friends and family. And they are less and less exposed to ways of solving problems, and communicating and the building of intimate relationships face-to-face.

In many respects, you – as the parent – have more on your shoulders as their model for communication than would have been so a generation or two ago. We tell children that 'sharing is caring', and this is true for us too – but in a different sense. If you don't already do so, you can share with your child how your day was (age-appropriately). For example, you can tell them:

'On my way home from work the sun came out and I was thinking about you – that was exactly the time you were outside, playing.'

'On the way back to the car, I saw this little dog and thought how cute you would find him'.

Share with them what you are doing now, how you solved a particular problem that day, what you are making for dinner, what you want to achieve in your work, your weekend, the holiday that you're going on, and so on. If you show them how to share during *relaxing* times, this will help them to share things with you during more *challenging* times.

Challenge them with the problem

I found that long before there is a conflict between a child and a parent, we have many options to react in a way that helps bring about a solution rather than generate more challenges.

When your child presents you with some issue that you find problematic, you do have choices. Many parents try to solve the issue at hand by offering options or solutions, perhaps when their child doesn't want to get out of the bath, or doesn't want to wear a coat on a cold day. You could react by saying '*You need to get out because it's story time*' or '*It's freezing outside and we don't leave the house without a coat*'.

These words might work, but if you feel they are going to create unnecessary conflict then you can say something that puts your child on the *solution* side – rather the problem one. Here are some suggestions:

> 'I see you're enjoying your bath. But we have a problem, because it's story time and you need to be in bed by seven-thirty.'

> 'You prefer not to wear your coat. I have a problem with that because it's very cold outside and you may catch a cold.'

That's it! Leave them with the problem.

In most cases, they come back with brilliant solutions. The examples above are real. In the first case, my client's child offered to stay in the bath for an extra five minutes and to have an extra-short story! In the second case, the daughter offered to wear an extra layer – a zipped fleece – and wear a coat, but left open.

Who says we need to offer the solutions? Let them be part of the *resolution* – not the problem.

The bonus in asking your child for solutions is that they learn that they can be part of resolving an issue. So, when your child is being the source of challenges – '*I want a play date*' (on a day when this is not possible) … '*I want you to take me to school*' (on the only day you can't do it) … '*I want this toy*' (when his friend has just started to play with it) – do not jump in to resolve it.

Briefly explain the situation and ask them for their opinion. They can be part of the solution, not the problem, which is a great skill to take with them into adulthood.

Be in touch

To communicate positively doesn't involve *only* face-to-face communication. When a parent works for long hours, leaves home before the children wake up, or has to work away from home, they can still keep relationships alive. Notes of appreciation, humour or love attached to their children's lunch box, or left under their pillow or on their iPad can all bring a smile to their day.

For older children, sending an email or text message to their mobile is a good option. The child discovers the note or message during the day, and feels special because you are thinking about them.

You don't need to be far away to surprise your child this way. Finding a note from a parent during the school day is always a magical moment. And for parents who need to travel, there are other ways to keep up the connection with their children. Here are some ideas:

- Try Skyping – it's a friendly programme that children can learn how to use to call you up (maybe from your partner's account for safety reasons).

- One of my colleagues suggests choosing a stone from the garden, marking or painting it in some way, and 'loading' it with kisses. You ask child how many kisses they want for each day and kiss the stone that number of times (and add more as extras). Then, whenever the child misses you they can 'charge' themselves up by 'downloading' the kisses. You can decide to have a stone each, and maybe decorate them. You could even put your perfume or aftershave on the one you leave with your child.

- Some parents leave a photograph of themselves beside their child's bed (for some children this is not a good option – if distracting themselves works well, seeing a photo can bring all their sadness back). For many, it makes them feel as if the parent is with them. Other ideas include giving them an old t-shirt or pyjama top for them to wear.

- One parent told me that she posts a letter to her child on the day she travels so her daughter receives it two days after the separation.

Whatever you choose to do, you can keep your relationship and communication alive when you are not physically present.

The message is that although we are physically apart, we are emotionally connected and can hold each other in our minds.

Twenty things children need to hear from their parents

I wrote down twenty things children need to hear from their parents. When my husband read the list, he said 'Can a husband also say these things to his wife?' to which I replied, 'Yes, but you have to add Number 21: The wife is always right!'

1. *It will be okay.*

2. *It's okay to cry.*

3. *You are allowed to feel angry.*

4. *I like being in your company.*

5. *You're okay the way you are. Be yourself.*

6. *You make sense and what you say makes sense (and when you are confused I will do my best to help you make sense of things).*

7. *Come and join me. Let's do something together.*

8. *I'm interested in hearing your opinion.*

9. *You are a special and worthy person.*

10. *You can tell me about your hurt and pain and I will be present with you (I will not collapse or make it about me).*

11. *There is no-one in the world that can take your special place in my heart.*

12. *I'm sorry.*

13. *Tomorrow is a new day.*

14. *I'm lucky to have you in my life.*

15. *Be kind – I will do my best to be a role model!*

16. *I'm not perfect, but I'm doing my best.*

17. *Don't dream big – dream great!*

18. *Playing is very important – but not on a screen.*

19. *Trying is more important than succeeding.*

20. *I love you.*

The battle of the homework

If *you* are the one who is worried about your child's homework, stressed for them that they will not get it done on time or do it tidily, and you keep reminding them, or nagging them, or arguing about it – you are probably not putting the responsibility for their homework on their shoulders. Homework is an issue that is raised often in my workshops. I hear parents discuss the reasoning behind their nagging. It may be related to the time and age in which we live and the academic pressure to excel, or to individual parent's anxieties (my child's success is *my* success) or cultural norms (he needs to be the best in his class). Whatever the reason, the power struggle with your children about homework doesn't teach them about taking responsibilities. Your relationship is more important than the doing of homework.

So, what's the alternative? Tell your children that their homework is between them and their teacher, and that they are old enough to be responsible for it. If they need help, you will be there for them, but the homework is theirs, not yours. For some children, thinking with them about the best time for them to do their homework is useful (it's best if not immediately after school, or before bed-time, or between various afterschool activities). Writing out a schedule to put above their desk or work table can help. It doesn't mean you are not going to help if your child asks a question, but if they don't understand how to do the homework it is important that they communicate this with their teacher. Inviting them – rather than you emailing the teacher on their behalf – to write their teacher about what they did not understand should help the teacher to guide them.

And what happens if they choose not to do their homework, parents often ask? This is the teacher's problem, not yours. Many children find it very stressful to go to school without their homework done. If you encourage them and they choose not to take on the responsibility, then anxiety in the morning before school might be a natural consequence. Add to this the fact that some teachers keep the children who didn't do their homework in the classroom to complete it, instead of enjoying play time.

This is how children learn to take responsibility for their own actions. You give them the support to do their homework, but it's their responsibility and their decision to do it. Can you see the difference? Once again, instead of being against them in a power straggle, you are with them, empowering them to develop. It also means you are working to collaborate with the school's expectations.

Your child's wisdom

You probably carry far too much on your shoulders, so why not invite your children to help? You can invite them to find solutions to everyday challenges. Feeling part of a problem – or part of the *solution* – is also related to the sense of belonging. I prefer to place the focus on being part of the solution.

Asking for your child's opinion, in a way that is age-appropriate, gives them the message that you appreciate and value them as wise people and that their opinion is important to you. This increases their contributions to the family, their creativity, and overall closeness.

Once you start asking them, you will be surprised by their creative thinking and ideas. Furthermore, when a child is part of the thinking process, they are much more engaged and cooperative in implementing the process.

For example, you can ask your child at the supermarket which items they think would be healthy to put in the fruit salad you will be eating later in the day. The more your child is involved in the shopping, the more they will be likely to help make (and eat!) it.

Remember, too, that not every question requires a discussion. Asking your child which tie fits the shirt you're wearing, or which trousers match a specific top all serve the same goal – they express that your child's opinion is valued. However, if you already know which tie you're going to wear, and are not really open to changing your mind – then don't ask for their opinion.

Only ask where their opinion can count.

- 3 -

Your smile can change
your child's brain!

*Sometimes your joy is the source of your smile, but sometimes
your smile can be the source of your joy.*
Thich Nhat Hanh

This chapter focuses on your body language and its affect on your relationships and your children.

The strength of a smile

Did you know that your smile is *actually* contagious? If you want to know more, get hold of a copy of Provire's article from 1992 called *Contagious laughter: Laughter is a sufficient stimulus for laughs and smiles.*

The part of your brain that is linked with the facial expressions of smiling resides in the cingulate cortex – an unconscious, automatic response area. Scientific studies have shown that the same area of the brain is activated when people see other people's faces when they are smiling or laughing – the positive emotions they get are the same as those when they smile themselves.

It seems that when our brains unconsciously process other people's actions, our neuronal patterns mirror them; in other words, our own brains experience the same emotion. We know about this from work carried out by Dimberg *et al.* in 2000. It's a lot like the contagious effect of yawning.

When you smile at your children, it's likely that they won't be able to help themselves from smiling back. Every time you smile or laugh together, their brain detectors lead them to return the smile. This is one way to create a relationship that allows both of you to release 'feel-good' chemicals (endorphins), which are known to increase the chances of you both living longer and lead healthier lives. As the researcher Provine says:

'The necessary stimulus for laughter is not a joke, but another person'.

Wants versus needs

When I ask children what they *want* from their parents when they spend time together, they say 'Fun'. And when I try to understand more about what they mean, they give me various explanations and examples. Interestingly, beneath all their answers is a common core *need*: they want to feel that you, their parent, *wants and likes* being with them. They don't want to feel that you *need* to do it (to make you feel better, for example), or that you're with them because you think it's what loving parents ought to do (again, to make you feel better), or because you haven't done it for a long time and they've been reminding you about it. They want you to do it *only* because you truly and utterly like and enjoy being with them. And how can they know that? Through your body language. When you are enjoying yourself, your body is relaxed, your facial expression is soft, and when you smile, you smile with your eyes. Also, you are *present*.

It means not forcing yourself to do something your child wants you to do, or something you resent doing. You have to find something that brings you joy as well – perhaps something you did when you were a child, or something you do now but want to share with your child. Are you enjoying Zumba? Great! Find a class for parents and children. You like programming technology? Then teach your child how to code their own game.

Bring them closer to your world, and try to visit their fun world too. Who knows, you might enjoy it!

Smile when you least feel like it

At the start of my career I remember working with a couple that I found very challenging. Their way of communicating with each other was stressful enough for any therapist, let alone one just starting out, like me. I discussed their case with my supervisor. Eventually, it became clear to me that I stood to learn an enormous amount from them.

One of the things my supervisor told me was: 'When you welcome the most challenging couples, receive them with a warm, empathic smile. They're the ones who need it the most'. I feel this is just as true with parents and their children.

We can smile a lot during the day, but children probably need our warmth and smile the most when they look like they least deserve it.

In every relationship, two can make a situation into a disaster, but we need only one person to improve it. Be that one! Give a warm, empathic smile when you ask them for things, when you say goodbye to them at school, when you say goodnight, and when you meet again.

Laughter therapy

Laugh a lot. Laugh more! Why not!?

When you laugh, those strong feel-good chemicals are released throughout your brain and body, and they can produce a feeling of euphoria and feel-good experiences. The same happens to your children when they laugh. But when you laugh *together,* your brain learns to associate the positive feelings *with* the other person – your child.

There are many other benefits for the body and mind, too, caused by the vibration of your body when you laugh, which releases tension and reduces anxiety. You can also provide a model for your child on how to lighten up situations using humour (never at their expense – only at yours). Children love it when their parents are playful with them. What is it that makes you laugh? Pillow fighting? Reading jokes from a book? A funny movie? Being silly? A game or an online clip? Show your child that it's fun to be an adult too! It isn't all about mortgages, household duties, and work! This way, they will have something to look forward while they are growing up.

If you find it difficult to laugh, have a look on-line. You will find many techniques to promote belly laughing. One of them involves standing with soft knees in front of someone else (an adult or child) and looking into each other eyes, then starting to make a noise with open mouths – something between a cough and a car starting to power up. Allow your voice to become louder and louder, and more intense, until out comes a long and fulsome belly laugh. Enjoy!

Attention time

Sometimes parents often feel pressurised to be somewhere on time, to leave the house in good time, or to organise something at home with several children and visitors. They try to get the family's attention so they can speed things up, but unintentionally they often create more chaos.

Here's a tip that can help increase focus under these circumstances. I learned it from my daughter's school-teacher. Whenever she claps her hands in a specific rhythm, all the children imitate her clapping and look at her. It's become built into them now, and is a very effective way to make thirty children silent within two seconds! I tried it out when I was organising my girls' birthday parties. I explained at the start that whenever I clapped my hands they should imitate the rhythm and turn their attention to me. It worked brilliantly. Not only do they love this 'game', but it also helps to stop everything that's going on so we can be clearer about the next step, and therefore speed things up.

The power of a glance

Do you already make eye contact when communicating with your children? Or did you raise your eyebrows when you read this question, saying 'of course' to yourself? Think again. Then think about how many times you speak to your child when your eyes are fixated on some kind of screen, whether a PC, iPad, smart phone, TV, or Kindle, or some other kind of device, like a tool you're sharpening, or a pan you're stirring, or a cupboard you're cleaning out? How many times do you actually *watch* your child playing in the playground, instead of catching up on e-mails or social media?

Parent–child connection cannot and should not be developing without eye contact. I have yet to hear a meaningful conversation between two people when one of them has their eyes on a screen. We say we don't want to miss a thing, but ironically we commonly pay the price of missing the moment.

Today's the day for you to decide that you'd like your children to remember the colour of your eyes when they grow up.

Children channel your calm

Your child's brain is very sensitive to the emotions of the people around them. They are alert and attuned to your state of mind, and they *react* to it.

It reminds me of watching one of the first parent–child research studies ever captured on video. The camera they used was huge, and the baby looked at the big strange box and the cameraman holding it with a frightened expression. His mother very naturally and calmly reassured him 'Ah, this is just a camera' and the child looked at her and said 'Ahh' as if he understood the meaning.

The child didn't understand what the words *meant*, but because of his mother's reassurance, he relaxed and continued to play, ignoring the camera. Her reaction signalled to him that it was safe, and then he reacted to her state of mind. If she had said something else with the same tone of voice and energy, it wouldn't have made any difference. The baby's brain picked up no sign of danger from his mother, and felt safe enough to move on.

You can use your tone of voice and your facial expressions and smile when interacting with your child so that they feel safe enough to develop themselves. If you find it difficult to do this, or know yourself to be very anxious, then seek support from your family and friends or a professional.

The look of love

A baby's brain develops most when it is in 'connection' with others. It doesn't develop by watching screens or people or characters on a screen, but through real-life interactions. When you look into your baby's eyes with soft, smiling eyes, seek out eye contact with them. Connect with them non-verbally with your warm gaze.

Generally speaking, baby boys tend to feel flooded or overwhelmed by an extended gaze. They might look away, or look distracted, before coming back. Baby girls, on the other hand, maintain eye contact more easily – without interruptions. I won't bore you with all the evolutionary explanations behind this phenomenon, but I will say that eye contact is equally important for boys and girls.

With boys, keep offering eye contact, and be present and available for them so they can safely explore around them when they feel overwhelmed, or over-stimulated, then return their attention to you once they are ready.

There's no age limit for making eye contact like this. In his book *Loving Hands: The Traditional Indian Art of Baby Massage*, Fredrick Leboyer invites parents to think about eye contact with their newborns during bath time.

Following his guidance regarding a 'holding position' he writes:

'Be passive. Entirely passive. Although totally aware. Do not try to direct. Do not interfere. Your baby is in his own element! Don't come between them. Let things happen. And watch! Watch how the whole body comes to life. And plays. Just watch, let it happen.'

- 4 -

Kindness goes a long way

Often the only thing a child can remember about an adult in later years, when he or she is grown, is whether or not that person was kind to him or her.
Billy Graham

This chapter explores ways to bring more kindness into our relationships with our loved ones. With the everyday pressures of life we sometimes forget that kindness is the most effective and healthy way to live. How can we bring more kindness to our daily interactions with our children? Start by committing to kindness. The tips below offer options for you to try out.

From the mouths of babes

Several years ago, when I was just about to leave home to give a lecture about positive parenting, one of my daughters, then four years old, asked me where I was going. I told her I was going to talk to other mums about positive ways to parent and asked her what she thought the most important thing was. She said: '*Just tell them to be kind. That's all!*'

Jim Henson, the American puppeteer and creator of the Muppets, said:

'The attitude you have as a parent is what your children will learn from, more so than what you tell them. They don't remember what you try to teach them, they remember what you are.'

I concur: your children will remember who you *are*. So, be kind!

Take it outside

The article called *What sleeping babies hear: A functional MRI study of interparental conflict and infants emotion processing* by Alice Graham and her co-authors suggests that even when infants are asleep, their brains are more than capable of taking in information from the tones of the voices around them. Moreover, infants who came from homes with a lot of conflict showed, *when they were asleep*, greater reactivity to negative tones of voice in certain areas of the brain – areas that are important later on for the child's ability to regulate emotions and function well.

In other words, if you want to argue loudly with your partner, it is not enough for your children to be asleep! You need to take your negativity elsewhere.

29

Buddha wisdom

*If you propose to speak, always ask yourself, is it true, is it necessary, is it kind?—**Buddha***

There's a lot to say for this piece of wisdom as it relates to parenting. We should keep reminding ourselves that saying *less* and doing it in a kind and respectful way will bring much more peace to our lives and joy to our parenting.

Parenting, as I said before, is a muscle that you need to exercise and stretch. One way to do this is to keep a diary of your parenting experiences. It is a great way to follow your own growth as a parent, and also to learn from about what works – and what doesn't – and to explore other options.

This week, try recording some of your interactions with your children, and explore whether they are in line with the quote above. Were they true? Were they necessary? Were they kind? If not, write down some alternatives, things that you could do or say instead.

Investing this time and thinking now will stretch your parenting muscle so it will be readily available to you in the future.

Emotional bank account

*One of the greatest questions to ask yourself at the end of the day is – if I were the only example my child has from whom to learn right from wrong, what would she have learned today?—**Dr Michelle Borba***

Not every day is full of positive experiences. We all share the experience of surviving a day of tantrums, stress and negativity – and I'm not talking only about the children! The good news is that tomorrow is a new day. Then we can address whatever issue or situation has arisen in a more positive and productive way. It's sometimes helpful to see your relationship with your child, and your child's emotional state, as your emotional *bank*.

The metaphor for a bank makes it clear: if we just pay out, without paying enough in, it's no surprise when the bank manager calls to air their concerns. If, on the other hand, we pay in regularly and from time to time take small amount out, the balance stays positive and healthy. It's the same with your emotional bank. If you are *generally* a warm, available and reliable parent, but lose your patience or have a difficult day, your emotional bank account is probably still in credit.

With regards to Dr Borba's question above, children can learn many positive things from their parents, including the fact that we make mistakes too, that we take responsibility for them, and that we work to resolve them.

Sow your values

There is a Buddhist metaphor that describes the seeds of love as a range of all emotions. The seeds that we *invest* in – the ones we water, take care of, nurture and focus on – are the seeds that will grow to be tall plants. If you imagine a circle representing the 'self'. The bottom part is the *store* of the self (the unconscious mind) and the upper part is the conscious mind. All the seeds are inside the store, and the ones that are nurtured grow the mind. The more time their shoots spend 'in the mind', the more their roots will expand in the store.

In the second part of the book, I explore options for working with what I call the 'negative seeds' – but for now let's keep thinking about all the positive seeds we would like to develop with and for ourselves – and our children. The simple rule is that the more you water a seed, the more it grows; when you stop watering it, it dies. It's finished. What are you watering in your child's garden? Are you watering appreciation, compassion, understanding and love? Every minute of the day, you can stop, reflect, be conscious, and react with those seeds in mind. We need to provide numerous opportunities for the positive seeds to grow, and when the seeds are 'in the mind' then we need to do whatever we can to keep them there for as long as possible.

How do you put this idea into practice? All you do is choose a seed you would like to water this week. How can you do that? You can notice it and describe it. You can encourage it. You can you 'model' it – act it out, or be it! Take, for example, the seed of kindness. Look out for kindness in your child and other people, and whenever you see it tell your child what you observed. Be careful not to make any interpretations – just describe what you see. Here are some everyday examples:

'You saw that the dog was sad and you gave him a hug although you were in a hurry. That was a kind thing to do.'

'It's very kind of you to ask whether I needed help.'

'She was very kind to lend me her book.'

'I appreciated the kindness those children showed to the new boy. What do you think about that?'

'That driver stopped the car so that we could cross the road safely. It was very kind of him.'

To grow the seed of kindness, simply notice kindness – and provide opportunities for it. Whatever seed it is you choose to grow this week, bring it to your consciousness throughout the week and see it flourish.

It's an educational road

You're in the kitchen and you see your daughter opening the cupboard doors under the sink where the cleaning products are – after you have already told her many times not to do so. What do you do? What is your instinct? (Don't over-think this.) What do you say? You may say with an emotion like anger 'I've told you a hundred times not to open that door – it's dangerous for you!' or 'I need to send you to your room to think about it,' or 'Why don't you listen?! I told you not to open those doors!'.

Messages like these will probably need to be repeated (and modelled) time and time again in the process of educating our children. However, when we react emotionally, we lose our children's attention. They switch from listening to being defensive, and the message is lost. But being assertive and kind will get the result we want more productively and quickly. There are alternative responses to the scenario above. First, meet your child at eye level, then say calmly and confidently:

> 'Daddy told you not to open that door. You can open this door instead, and see what's inside.'

Short and sweet. Rather than responding only with 'No', you have offered an option to take their curiosity to a different place. No shaming. And no blaming. Kind and clear.

Play-date patience: remembering the real you

I've noticed that when I'm short on patience, I can react sharply to my children. One of them isn't too bothered by this, but the other is much more sensitive about the way I communicate. I've also noticed that if I'm hosting one of my children's friends for a play-date, then I'm much more pleasant – even when I'm short on patience. If the friend is making a mess with paint, for example, I'll encourage them to fix the situation in a nice way.

So why is it that we hold ourselves to a higher standard with other people – even strangers – but not to the ones who are most important to us?

When talking about this with a couple in a session once, they suggested that the way we are at home is the 'real' us – we are free to be ourselves. This begs the question, then: can't we be real and be ourselves in a kind way? Why, when speaking with a stranger in a kind way, is it not the 'real' us? To the people who are most important to us we allow ourselves much more leeway than we should.

So I remind myself of this whenever I can, and when I'm short on patience I imagine myself talking to a stranger when I communicate with my children. I'd prefer them to remember this me as the 'real' me.

The "Thank you!" way

Observing several teachers at nurseries and primary schools over the years has helped me understand what works best with children. There are the teachers who say: '*Don't disappoint me on this trip*' or '*I'm so disappointed!*' or '*Did I ask you to do that? So why are you doing it?*' or '*Why aren't you tidying up with your class?*'.

Then there are the other types, who use more respectful and positive language, and say 'thank you' at every opportunity:

'Thank you for being such a wonderful class during the trip.'

'I'm so proud of you today!'

'Can you help me with this? Thank you!'

'Good listening to instructions. Can you wait for your turn?'

'I'm so proud of all of you for sitting so nicely. Give yourselves a clap.'

I've also noticed that the latter type of teachers use more questions than statements. For example:

'Thank you for bringing me this drawing. Would you like to help your friends to tidy up?'

'Do you want to put the plates in the big box?'

The difference might not seem too dramatic, but after many observations over a long time, I have come to a number of conclusions. The teachers who say how disappointed they are reduce motivation in their classes, which results in a continuing sense of the teacher's disappointment. The teachers who use appreciations and respectful words of 'thank you' and 'please' achieve far more cooperation and have reason to feel proud of their classes. Not only this, but the teachers who use questions more than statements motivated the children to cooperate more. I have to say, it was much more fun and relaxing to sit in on their classes.

And when we feel relaxed, we have energy to be curious to learn and develop. Whatever your child's experience at school, you can bring this tip into your home.

Thank you.

Don't play the shame game

The smallest act of kindness is worth more than the grandest intention—Oscar Wilde

Coming from a country where people need to learn to say 'Thank You' more often, I am very impressed with the English culture of manners, and people are generally kind to each other. However, I sometimes hear parents trying to teach their children to be polite and I cannot ignore the dissonance between the lesson the parents are trying to give and the way they deliver it.

Some shout hysterically and aggressively (*Say thank you! ... Did you say thank you?*) even when the child has already said it! Some shame the child into saying it (*You're old enough to know better ... Why didn't you say thank you? ... I didn't hear you say thank you*). Some even say thank you on behalf of the child with a tone of voice and attitude that expresses sarcasm or anger or disappointment.

We cannot teach politeness by being mean!

We cannot teach politeness and respect to others by not acting politely to our children in the process of their learning.

So, how can we do it, you may wonder? Look:

> Child: 'Mum can I have a cup of water?'
>
> Parent: 'Please can I have a cup of water?' *(without sarcasm or a negative tone of voice)*
>
> Child: 'Please can I have a cup of water?'

Never embarrass your child in front of other people. You can kindly and gently ask if they want to say thank you. If they are young or struggle with that, then you can say 'thank you' on their behalf and talk to your child about your expectations when it's just the two of you and you're in a good space.

- 5 -

What you see from here, you do not see from there

Most misunderstandings in the world could be avoided if people would simply take the time to ask 'What else could this mean'?
Shannon L. Alder

There is a huge amount of freedom that comes to you when you take nothing personally.
Miguel Ruiz

Understanding your child's view of the world can change the way you connect with them. Here I describe the ways you can enter your child's 'inner world'.

Understanding the code

I start my positive parenting workshops with this game. I ask for two volunteers to leave the room. Within the group, I hide an object. When the volunteers return, they ask the whole group or particular individuals 'Yes/No' questions to find the object. Sounds easy, right? But there's a catch. I guide the group to answer their questions using specific codes for 'Yes' and 'No'. The rules of the game are made very clear to the group, and all their answers make sense once you know the code, but the two volunteers don't know it and soon they feel misled, frustrated, angry, and helpless. A level of frustration is always there even though it is just a game.

In many ways this is how parents and children communicate, because they speak different languages! And when we don't understand each other, it creates negative feelings. In my workshops this can be funny because we know it's a game. For our children, however, it's daily life. For example, children might say their tummy hurts when they feel anxious or nervous. They may complain about having boring homework when in fact they find it too hard to complete. They might ask what you do with the dead fish you find in the fish tank, because they are concerned about the death of a relative. Or they might tell you about another sick child at school who waited for his parents to pick him up, just to be assured that you will be able to pick them up if needed. This is not manipulation – this is how they experience the world and how they make sense of things. Try to learn their language, and to work out what your child is trying to tell you.

A world of giants

It is said that 'to the world you may be one person, but to one child you may be the whole world'. So how do toddlers experience us? First, we are huge! We are giants! Our body is gigantic, our bags too, and our plates piled with food. What they see from their height and perspective is very different from what we see. Have you ever been back to a place you frequented as a child – and found to your surprise how much smaller it was than you remembered?

Imagine spending a day on your knees. This is how toddlers experience their environment. From their perspective, they really see, feel and experience 'reality' differently.

You can take this into account when you plan your child's room. Some parents buy their young children a double bed, because they want them to have space and comfort – without realising that from the child's perspective this can be overwhelming. A large bed, in their eyes, might make it difficult for them to contain their fears– it can be scary! These parents obviously have the best of intentions, yet the children end up being afraid to go to sleep. Replacing the bed with a small, age-appropriate one provides psychological safety for young eyes and minds, and can make all the difference. They can see the edge of the bed, they know where it starts and where it ends, so they have a sense of control that helps them to contain their fears.

Why do they act the way they act?

Many children resist doing what their parents say. In many cases, when you experience your child's resistance, it isn't about *you*. They're resisting as part of their own development. Yes. I know, that statement doesn't make sense, but let me explain.

You want to read a new book to your children, but they insist on hearing a book you've already read out loud over a hundred times! Why is it they keeps wanting the same book? Or to go on the same slide in the playground? Or do the same puzzles time after time? The reason is because they still get something from that book or activity, or they are in the process of working things out about it. This is their developmental task. With books, for example, they learn about constancy, a sense of things, prediction, language, a deeper understanding of the story. When they are very young, children don't actually know that the end of the story will be the same every time! And each time they read or hear the same story, they understand something new. They will keep asking for the same book until their developmental needs are satisfied.

So, instead of being concerned about it, stay with them in the experience. Don't rush them to move on. Trust that they will guide you.

The quick step

I was walking along the street with my family when the elder one, then seven years old, started to walk in a funny way. I asked her in an amusing tone what she was doing. She replied that she was imitating her younger sister, then just three. My husband and I looked at the younger child's legs and saw that for her to keep up with our pace she needed to walk three steps for every one of ours. She was doing the quick step on a regular basis! So we all tried to imitate her walk. What can I say? It was tiring! Small, quick steps take a lot of effort.

This doesn't mean children don't need to walk, and I actively encourage parents to reduce the use of buggies and pushchairs for children aged two to two and a half, and to give it away (!) before the child reaches three. It's important for children to walk, not to be carried, for their physical and emotional health, but I hear many parents say that their children don't like to walk.

So? Does that mean we have to carry them or push them in a buggy until they are five? No, it doesn't.

Here are a few things I found helpful when walking with the family.

- Be interested in what they see and experience from their perspective (and eye level) to create conversation and connection, so that the walking becomes a source of connection, rather than a physical challenge.
- When your child says they are exhausted and cannot walk any further, say something like 'Let's see if we can reach the next lamp before I count to five.' Amazingly, that can get them running like lions!
- Try passing imaginary energy between each other – like a special power – between your hands. This way you can 'give' each other energy when ever needed.
- Try varying the way you walk in a way that is playful – try backwards, skipping, or walking like a specific animal.

We don't always have the time and energy to invest in these ideas, but whenever you are in a good space, try it out and keep developing your own tricks.

A rocky gift

When a child gives you a gift, even if it is a rock they just picked up, exude gratitude.
It might be the only thing they have to give, and they have chosen
to give it to you—Dean Jackson

I love this quote. Every parent will recognise the situation when their child picks up some rubbish (that is, in the parent's view) from the floor and offers it as a gift. This quote really brings it home for me. And it brings us back to the child's perspective. When my daughter was young and she became angry with me or her father, she would say, 'I will not invite you to my birthday party'. My initial reaction was to say 'I'm the one who organises your parties, so if I'm not invited there won't be any party'. I saw the disappointment and anger in her face, so I consciously went back to the basics – to see it from her perspective! From her perspective, her birthday party was probably one of the most important events she knew. To use this threat in this way was just her way of showing us how upset she was. So I replaced the unnecessary fact that I usually responded with a comment about how she felt:

> 'Ah, I can see that you're very upset and right now you don't want to invite me to your party'.

She then said more about how she felt and we took it from there (more tips on that to follow). Luckily, she gave me many more opportunities to practice this kind of interpretation, so it became more natural for me to react in a productive way.

Planned screaming

Children express themselves with their voices. They may shout – sometimes from excitement and other times from fear. Screaming is not so bad for them. So before you tell them not to shout – think twice. When they are very young, the sounds they make are important for developing their voice, and are also a great way to release aggression and anxiety. While we don't want them to scream all day, we can help them express themselves in an appropriate way and at an appropriate time.

So-called 'transformational breathing' is a way to use sounds to release strong emotions. You can make use of this at home by telling your children that you can do it together instead. You all take a full breath in and make a strong sound – or scream – until you have no more air in your lungs. Then inhale deeply again and do it again. After doing this four times, the vibrations in your body should produce a calmer state of mind. So rather than stopping your children with another exclamation of 'No shouting!', join in with them. Obviously this isn't appropriate in a public place (if a waiter asks you to leave the restaurant, don't blame me!), but you can do it at home or in the park, or to indicate that you understand them:

'I can see how excited you are – you really want to scream with excitement. You know what? As soon as we're back in the car let's take a deep breath and scream!'

Don't give the third degree

You pick up your child from school. You're very keen and interested to know how her day was. What do you say? Most parents welcome children after school with endless questions: '*How was your day? … Who you did you play with? … Why are you sad? … What did you eat for lunch? … Did you tell your teacher that?... Why you are so grumpy? Do you think it's nice to pick you up from school when you're like this?*'.

And what would most children answer? Probably just 'Yes' or 'No' or 'I don't know'. Now imagine yourself in this child's shoes. You're back home after a very busy and stressful day at work. You had to deliver a difficult presentation, you had disagreements with a colleague, and your boss placed yet more responsibility on your shoulders. You couldn't wait to get home. You open the door, desperate to have a coffee and some quiet time, but before this happens your partner comes in from the other room, looking very cheerful, and asking you: 'How was your day?'. You answer 'Busy'. He replies, '*Why are you sad? What did you eat for lunch? Did you tell your boss that —? Why didn't you tell your colleagues —? Why you are so grumpy?*'.

How would this make you feel?

Now imagine yourself coming home again – same situation. You open the door. Your partner sees your face, smiles, comes over to you and gives you a long hug, then says 'It looks like you had a long day. I'll make some coffee. I'm happy you're home'.

Can you see the difference?

In which situation would you be more likely to feel understood and want to share?

Parenting expert Doctor Haim Ginott says in his book *Between Parent and Child*: 'In most situations, making statements is preferable to asking questions'. This week, then, when picking up your children from school, welcome them with a smile, and a hug and say:

'I'm so happy to see you!'

That's it! If you want to comment on a good mood, then add something like:

'I see you're very happy/excited today.'

Let them choose when, where, and what to tell you about their day.

Traffic-light danger

I went to meet Mrs Smith, a year-one teacher at a private school in London. We arranged the meeting because I work with the family of a girl in her class and wanted to understand more about her own challenges with the girl. I noticed a large triangle on the classroom wall, divided into three colours – green at the bottom, yellow in the middle, and red at the pointed top. I was curious about it, because I understood it was for encouraging positive behaviour. The teacher pointed out that it was like traffic lights – green for good behaviour, yellow for a warning, and red for negative behaviour.

Now let's see this from a child's point of view. First, climbing up the triangle relates to increasingly problematic behaviour. Second, two-thirds of the chart is negative – yellow was a warning, which is not a positive thing. A method like this actually encourages negative behaviour because that's the focus of most of the chart. There are not many options for progress, or for encouraging positive behaviour. There must be a better way to go about it. At another school, I saw a long chart, in the form of a photographic film strip, with seven colours, each of which had a statement printed on it. From the bottom up they said:

- 'Talk to Parents' on black.
- 'Teacher's Choice' on light blue.
- 'Think About It' on dark blue.
- 'Ready to Learn' on green.
- 'Good Work' on yellow.
- 'Great Job' on orange.
- 'Outstanding' on red.

At the start of every day, all the children's name tags are placed on green (Ready to Learn) and the teacher uses the chart very cleverly to encourage good behaviour. It gives the children more options to shine, to progress, to develop, and there's an equal opportunity to be on the positive side or the negative side, or to stay neutral in the middle. This allows each child to correct their misbehaviour more quickly and with less shame (the equivalent of being in the red, or consistently in the yellow in the first chart). On this chart, when a child's name climbs upwards, it represents outstanding behaviour. So, from your children's perspective (not yours!), and in the family situation rather than the classroom, would they feel that your focus and attention are unbalanced like the traffic-light chart with respect to time-outs, and so on, or would they feel that there's an equal opportunity to shine as with the film-strip?

The camera doesn't lie

If you want to learn a vast amount about your parenting, you should use a video camera at home. Watching myself in a home video provided insights about my children's experiences that were absolute gems. I can still remember when my younger one learned to walk. She was just ten months old and physically petite, and I excitedly asked my husband to film it.

Watching the footage later, I saw how excited I had been as I encouraged her to take her first few steps. Then her sister, four years older, wanted me to watch her rolling over. I said 'Yes of course. When she finishes her steps it will be your turn'. After several steps, she fell on her bottom – very pleased with herself – and I told my elder daughter that it was her turn. She started to roll over, with the intention of rolling over several times in a row, but in the middle of this, my little one stood again, barely balancing, and tried for the second time to walk on her own. I immediately called to my husband 'Look, look! She's walking!!'

It was only when watching the video that I saw my elder daughter's reaction – a very quiet and gentle disappointment that I was not 'present' for her. No aggression to her sister or to me, no tantrum, no drama, just quietly looking at me.

I can tell you this was very painful for me to see. I was so sure I was a balanced parent, giving my attention to all, noticing and being attuned to everyone's needs, but the video reminded me that it is not about what I think I do, but how my child experiences me.

The video helped me see things from her point of view, and enabled me to be more empathic and understanding. Since then, I've tried to remember that when one of my children achieves a milestone, the other still has a need to be seen.

What children experience in their world might be very different from what we experience.

The point is that I, and you, might not be the parent we think we are. Film yourself from time to time in order to be curious and grow your understanding.

Beyond behaviour: seeing the schema

Your three-year-old child is 'driving' his sit-on truck in quick circles at home, over and over again, making noises, and apparently playing quite roughly. What do you say? What's your instinctive reaction?

For many parents, the immediate response is to say something like '*Not so fast!*' or '*Can't you relax a bit?*' or '*Stop playing like that!*'. Does that sound familiar?

When observing Ruthie Akainyay, a teacher at a Montessori nursery in London, one little boy was doing exactly that, in the garden. He was driving a toy car, sitting inside and moving it by flapping his legs, but he was going very fast, which was quite rough for a space with other children around.

Ruthie: 'Daniel, are you driving a bus? Is it the C11?'

Daniel: 'Yes, it is a bus, but not the C11.'

Ruthie: 'So which one are you?'

Daniel: 'The 268!'

Ruthie: 'Where are you going?'

And she continued to add 'narrative' to his play. With the narrative he processed new information, making sense of things, and he also decreased his speed. She turned to me and said:

'He's at the schema stage of understanding wheels. It's a phase when he will be obsessed and fascinated by everything on wheels. So whatever we want to teach him, we use his language – of wheels – whether we're teaching him numbers, narrative, or phonics. So in this situation instead of saying "Stop" or "Why're you doing this?", I attach a narrative to his play.'

Can you recognise when your child is trying to master something? And the phase or schema your child is experiencing? Perhaps its filling cups of water, trying to control a pen, or mastering a spoken sound?

Try adding a narrative to their behaviours to help them make sense of the world around them.

- 6 -

Encourage conversation
— not interrogation

Listen earnestly to anything your children want to tell you, no matter what. If you don't listen eagerly to the little stuff when they are little, they won't tell you the big stuff when they are big, because to them all of it has always been big stuff.
Catherine M. Wallace

We all talk with our children, but are we encouraging conversation – or are we interrogating them? In this chapter, you will explore different tools that encourage children to share their feelings and experiences.

Space, space, space

A mother once told me that her daughter Zoe didn't share anything with her. Zoe didn't like to talk, and her mother felt that she was holding her emotions inside. Then she came with Zoe to see me and we video-recorded the session. It was enlightening for her to see her reactions to every one of her daughter's attempts to talk. Although it was with the best of intentions, she spoke for Zoe, she reacted defensively to her comments, and she corrected (another word for criticised) her memory as she recounted things to me.

If your children are like Zoe – not big on sharing – you need to be extra aware of their need for space and safety. Let them lead the conversation by giving them the time and space to explore their feelings, thoughts and beliefs. And give them enough time ... I love it when parents come back to me and say that they used this waiting approach, and just before the point of giving up and saying something, their child spoke out and deepened the conversation. Don't try to ask them what they said or what they did. Don't use the space to 'educate' them on their behaviour or responsibilities. If you feel your child is struggling with something, you might ask them:

'What do you need to resolve this issue?'

The premise is that your child is active in this process – you are not providing answers. Even though it can be painful for you to see your child struggle, with sufficient time and space they will find the answers and inner wisdom to resolve most of their challenges.

Your job is to be alongside them in this task. By attempting to solve a problem for them, by rushing in with a solution, you deprive them of the opportunity to develop trust in their own sense of 'agency'.

Face feelings

Too often, parents say to me 'Why talk about feelings? Doesn't it make things worse?'. No, it doesn't. Imagine your child as a pressure-cooker. The heat inside builds and builds. If you use a pressure-cooker you'll know that it's very dangerous to open at the end of cooking – it can blow up in your face!

So what do you do? You release the pressure slowly, in a safe and controlled manner. It's the same with children and their feelings. Ignoring how they feel means things *will* blow up at some point in time, and that's not healthy for the child – or your relationship.

I'd like to list some of the reasons I believe it's important to talk about feelings:

- You, as the parent or caregiver, can help your child to express how they feel in healthy and appropriate ways so that they can self-regulate their emotions. In other words, they can talk about how they feel rather than act out with behaviours like aggression, attention-seeking or depression.

- Children who know how to express how they feel are more likely to grow up to be more confident, to have good social skills, to know that asking for help is a strength and not a weakness, and experience less mental health problems like depression and anxiety.

- Most importantly, talking with your child about feelings provides you with an opportunity to learn more about their inner world and opens a safe path for them to explore their challenges.

This fundamental skill of emotional bonding is extremely worthwhile, and it will continue to deepen as your child grows. I have produced a short film called *The Feelings Cake*, in which I show how to create a fun and effective art project with your child that will encourage you both to talk about feelings. You can find this on *YouTube* (the details are in the *Resources* section at the back of the book).

A key point to be made is that talking with your children about feelings is most effective when there is no conflict between you. Caught up in the heat of a tantrum, your child will find it very challenging to cooperate with sharing their feelings (there is more about this in *Part Two*).

Practising your talking skills in no-conflict situations builds healthy habits that are easy to follow in times of need.

Send an invitation

When you want to initiate a conversation with your child, *invite* them – by asking if this is a good time for them. Children have their own worlds and interests, which is why you should check that they are available, or whether they would prefer to talk later. This gives the message that you respect their space.

And this way – more often than not – your children will want to hear what you have to say. If a child says it is not a good time, invite them to initiate the talk over the next day or two. It's important for you to *involve* them in what happens between you.

If you see that something is bothering your children and they are not willing to talk about it, you can tell them:

> 'I can see something's bothering you. I'm here for you. Whenever it's right for you to share, I'll be here for you'.

Saying this in a kind and compassionate way will give the message that you *are* there to be with them whenever it's right for *them*.

Cultivate curiosity

Every episode of parent–child communication can be used to either empower children or to learn something new about them.

In one of my lectures, I ask parents what they would say when their child asks: 'Dad, why are the trees without leaves?'. They usually provide a long, reasonable and factual answer. Which is great. Yet there are other options.

You could instead respond:

> 'That's an interesting question. What do you think?'

You'll be surprised to find that children have their own guesses for every question they come up with. They just need the space to explore, so if you can hold your answer for a little longer, you will learn something new about the way they think.

Another option is to direct them to information in a book, or together you could look for an answer on the internet. Do this after they have provided their own answer. Aim to acknowledge their curiosity, and empower them!

The license to "be"

When you talk with your child, the message should be that they are okay as they are. That they make sense. If your child expresses sadness, anxiety or fear, make sure you have physical contact with them.

This will help them feel more secure and safe. Sometimes a hug is worth more than comforting words, and your body language should express openness and willingness. What does that look like? A softened face, lots of eye contact, slow breathing and warm eyes.

Let them talk, and do not interrupt.

The message you are getting across is that they are allowed to feel what they feel and to express it in appropriate ways. We want to encourage, support, be kind and be respectful.

We want to show that we care. We cannot do that if we are criticising or dismissing their feelings.

"Thank you for telling me"

Sometimes when children share with us how they feel, we have the urge to react. If it's about us (they might tell you they were really upset when you yelled at them the previous day, or that they were sad when they heard you and your partner arguing), we often react by offering explanations, or reasons, or apologies. But when we do that, we shift the focus from how the child feels on to ourselves.

Instead of doing this, try to reflect and mirror what you've heard your child say, and thank them for sharing their thoughts with you. Here's an example:

'I understand that yesterday you heard us argue and it made you sad. Is there more you want to tell me about that?'

Mirror your child's answer (repeat it back in your own words) and follow with:

'Thank you for sharing with me how you feel.'

And *stop there*! Think about it, digest it, and (if really necessary) address the matter with your child at a different time. From these small conversations you give your children the message that they can share how they feel in a safe way and that you are strong enough to deal with whatever it is with them. And in the future, when more challenging situations arise, sharing how they feel will have become second nature to them. Just remember to say:

'Thank you for telling me. Now I know how you feel.'

Language stimulations are good – but your approach is better

Research on language development indicates that children do not learn vocabulary from so-called 'stimulation' of words and ideas. The children who have the widest vocabulary are those who were *listened to* the most by the adults around them.

To stress this point, it isn't how many words they hear that develops their language, but their use of words, their enjoyment of words and an appreciation of their power that keeps them in the memory.

And this all relates to *doing* versus *being* – it's not what you *do* with your child, it is how you *are* with them.

The *being* is the most important thing for their development. Being calm and relaxed, enjoying your children's presence and doing 'nothing' (not entertaining, correcting or educating them) is what matters. In truth, simply being *present* is the greatest gift you can give your child.

Are your comments "expanding" or "closing"?

When your child shares something with you, whether its positive or challenging for him, your reaction can go either way, to expand or close the connection. By expand, I mean inviting your child to a new way of thinking, in a way that raises them up, with a comment that empowers their strengths and their self, that trusts their judgment and ability.

The opposite is 'closing' the connection, which means saying something that humiliates them or puts them down, that questions their understanding or ability, or criticises their behaviour or character (*But why did you do that? ... How could you think that? ... You don't need to feel upset... It's just the same – like last time ...*). These are all examples of closing conversations. They invite defensiveness.

In contrast, raising up – expanding – doesn't include hidden criticisms, it simply reflects the child's situation and opens a future possibility. Expanding options could include:

'This sounds like a tricky situation. What would you like to do?'

'How can I support you with this?'

'I remember how you solved the problem with Rachel. What did you learn that might be helpful now?'

Listen long (and talk short)

When children speak about negative feelings they encounter in a game or story, for instance, ask them what they would do if they have ever felt that way, and what they did, or might do, to make themselves feel better. This gives perspective to the challenging emotion, and brings it to the here and now. It can also highlight the fact that they coped well with this feeling in the past.

If they share something positive, you could ask when they felt that way before, or when they made someone else feel that way. This empowers their ability to affect others. It's also the place for sharing memories of your feelings from childhood – or now, as adults. Children love hearing about our experiences.

The main point is to listen long and talk short. When parents listen to their children speaking about negative emotions such as loneliness, hurt and sadness, they often find it upsetting and consciously (or unconsciously) try to dismiss the child's feelings (*Oh, you don't really hate your sister*), or to fix things (*Just don't be her friend if this is how she makes you feel*) or to come to the rescue (*I'll talk to him and your teacher about that!*). None of these reactions invite children to explore how they feel in a safe way. You also want to help them to develop resilience; that is, the capacity to know that uncomfortable feelings can be survived – even if it's not always easy.

What I often hear from children (and from adults about their own childhoods) is that all they really wanted was to be heard by someone who cared enough. Children do not want you to save them, or to tell them what to do, or do anything, or to explain why things happen to them. They do not need you to have all the answers. They just want to know that you are there, with them, so they are not alone with their feelings.

You can repeat what your child is saying to you, just to validate that you've understood what they wanted to express. Knowing they are not alone gives them the courage to cope with their feelings in a healthy way. As I said – talk short and listen long. And check what you said afterwards: When I talked, did I give advice and instructions? Did I show my understanding?

For me, this process is especially challenging. At my clinic, people pay to hear my advice, but at home I need to keep my advice to myself! It is difficult, but it's not impossible!

Mirroring and your child's brain

A voice without echo dies—Unknown source

The well-known paediatrician and psychoanalyst Donald Winnicott said that the parent or main caregiver is the first 'mirror' of the baby. The baby sees himself in its parent's face and expressions. But how does the baby know if this is how the parent feels, or whether it's a reflection of the baby's feelings?

Parents usually exaggerate their expressions when reflecting their baby's feelings. Take a look at the parents of babies and toddlers in the playground. When the baby giggles with happiness, the parent reflects this back, with extra expressions of happiness. When a toddler falls down and cries in pain, the parent mirrors their sadness with their face (unless it's the type of parent who dismisses children's feelings).

This process of reflecting a child's inner emotions, also known as 'attunement', has a strong influence on the developing brain. Attuned parents reinforce positive brain circuits. When parents don't regularly reflect back emotions such as joy, whether through a lack of mirroring or because they disregard joyful behaviour, the patterns in the brain's circuit for joy are not reinforced.

What is important to know, as I discussed in an earlier chapter, is that the brain uses the same nerve pathways to create an emotion as it does to respond to the same emotion, thus if there isn't enough attunement to joy, for example, then the child develops a passive reaction to joy.

Attuned parents provide their baby's brain with experiences that hardwire the inner feeling of joy. This regular mirroring strengthens the natural connections of the circuit so that babies learn how to create and experience joy for themselves.

This starts really early in life, even before conscious memory begins, so every time you reflect back your child's emotions, you truly are reinforcing appropriate and healthy connections in their brain.

Mirroring is key to development of the self

My sister-in-law sent me a clip of herself interacting with her four-month-old son. It was lovely to see the natural mirroring that she provided. He giggled and she giggled, he laughed and she laughed, he stopped laughing and she stopped laughing. As Winnicott states, a parent's ability to know, represent, and mirror an infant's experience back at them is *fundamental* to its capacity to represent and understand its own inner world.

Unfortunately, parents somehow lose this ability as the child grows. At Imago, we believe that reflecting back the child's experience is fundamental to his or her healthy development.

'Mirroring' means repeating their words as well as their energy, tone and expression, all with the intention of connecting and helping the child feel seen and heard. Appropriate mirroring results in the experience of 'being seen' and creates a sense of 'I exist'.

In the week ahead, look out for every opportunity to practice mirroring your children. It isn't the same as 'copying' but involves reflecting aspects of their feelings, words and expressions. Some children will benefit most if you repeat every word they say, word for word, but some will prefer you to rephrase their words. Others will only require non-verbal mirroring, with empathic eyes, facial expressions and comments like:

'Mmm ... I understand'.

The goal is to practice mirroring your child until it feels as natural as it used to be between you.

At Imago, we explain about the ideal dialogue between parents and children with the help of the acronym MOVE which stands for:

M irror

O ver (and over)

V alidate

E mpathise.

After practising mirroring as described above, you can begin on the next level, which is validation.

VALIDATION

Validating involves seeing the situation from your child's perspective, so it makes sense that this is what they feel, say or do. After appropriate validation, your child experiences your understanding of their reality. Saying 'You make sense ...' doesn't mean that you agree or experience the same perspective as them, or that you are going to permit whatever it is your child wishes, just that you acknowledge and validate their perspective. These are examples of validation:

'It makes sense that you would prefer to play in the playground than go home!'

'Of course you'd like to eat ice-cream all day!'

EMPATHY

Having empathy means acknowledging the emotional state of another person. When we try to speculate on how a child might be feeling, we help them feel connected – to themselves and to us – and understood. Expressing empathy looks like this:

'I can imagine you might be feeling disappointed.'

'I bet you're feeling excited!'

Note that the feelings do not need to be explained or justified – you can avoid reasons and simply name the emotion. Parents sometimes worry that they will miss the emotion or create an emotion that isn't there, but I can assure you that most children will clarify what they are feeling.

One mother told me 'It didn't work. I told him "Oh, I can imagine that you feel angry"' and he said "No, I'm furious!"'. This shows that her child knew how he felt and made it perfectly clear to her. You don't need to get the feeling right, which is why you *offer* a name for the feeling (*I can imagine ... I guess ...*) rather than a conclusion.

Practising MOVE will help you master this skill. You'll see a change in the energy and connection between you and your children when they feel noticed, existing, and seen.

Don't wait for challenges before you practise – as you will know by now, it is much more productive and effective to start mastering any parenting skill in problem-free situations so that you react more naturally when a problem arises.

- 7 -

Teach your children
to trust their instincts

Your job as a parent is not to make your child's way smooth, but rather to help her develop inner resources so she can cope.
Ellyn Satter

Behind every young child who believes in himself is a parent who believed first.
Matthew Jacobson

Growing up means children have to make their own decisions, especially when they are not in the presence of their parents. Here I will discuss the ways young children can learn to trust their own judgement, so they are more likely to have the confidence to go with their own instincts, rather than be swayed by pressure from their peers.

"I am amazing!"

One of the things my children learnt at nursery school was to acknowledge their strengths. Their teacher, Ruthie, started each day with a 'registration' song to welcome each child. Then every child put their right hand on the left side of their chests (where their hearts are), and Ruthie tapped her hand on her own heart and said: 'I am kind'. The children followed her, tapping and saying 'I am kind'. Then she said 'I am …' and waited for suggestions from the children. A child might say 'I am brave' and the rest would follow with 'I am brave', or 'I am beautiful', 'I am strong', 'I am loved' or 'I am happy'.

Isn't this a lovely way to start the day?

What I love about what Ruthie did is that she used this in many situations. When one child knocked over another's tower of blocks, she reminded them 'I am kind' and everyone repeated the action and the words. When she told them a story and the character needed to be brave she reminded them 'I am brave' and they all imitated her. It very quickly brought a positive and encouraging energy to the room and to each child's self.

There's no reason why we can't bring this into our own family life. Why not to go off to sleep with 'I am amazing!'?

The magic of mistakes

How many times a day do parents say '*Be careful! ... Stop! ... Be careful with that plate! ... Be careful of the table corner! ... Be careful or you'll fall!*' and so on. Sometimes, when we say '*Stop!*' and '*Careful!*' we take responsibility for a skill or knowledge that our children need to learn and master by themselves.

When one of my children is close to a hot oven or running by a road, I say loudly and clearly:

'Careful. The oven is hot.'

'Stop. It's a busy road.'

When they hear the word 'careful' or 'stop', they stand still. I take responsibility for that moment and for teaching them how to take care of themselves in the future. But we should only do this when our children are in significant danger, because we do not want to prevent them from developing their own abilities and awareness. After all, we're not with them at school and we want them to *learn* the necessary skills to be safe without us, and to trust their own judgement.

The next time your child is playing under the table and you can see they're about to bang their head, say gently:

'Erica, be aware of the table above your head'.

This raises their awareness, but leaves them to judge what to do with the information. With this approach, they may experience some minor injuries, but we all know that there is no better way to learn than first-hand experience. We want our children to grow into adults who can trust their instincts and abilities, and this is one way that we can promote that.

Indulge the inner artist (silently)

Every child is an artist. The problem is how to remain an artist once we grow up—*Pablo Picasso*

When you watch your children drawing or painting, keep all your suggestions to yourself! Telling them which colour they need to use, or 'correcting' something they are painting from their imagination makes it *your* art and not theirs.

When you next feel an urge to say something, just take a piece of paper and make your *own* art! And remember, we can all learn a thing or two from our little artists.

Let them explore their own way

I remember dropping my daughter off at nursery one morning and chatting with a friend of mine by the door, who had a very active four-year-old boy. She suddenly stopped talking when she noticed her son had put a chair up on to a table, and was clearly going to climb up so that he could look through a high window. She was just about to call out to him to say it was dangerous when the teacher, Ruthie (who I mentioned earlier), reached out and touched her hand and said:

'I see him. If it becomes dangerous, I'll tell him. He is just exploring and he is safe'.

The boy, unaware of all the drama, climbed up on to the table and then the chair on top of it, had a quick look outside (the window was closed and safe) then clambered back down, put the chair back in its place and moved on to exploring the room. I tell you this because it reminds me that sometimes it is our fear that stands between us and letting our children be. In the name of protection, we say 'No' too many times during the day. Some 'No's are necessary, but others are more about our own concerns about social rejection, safety, inner anxiety, to name but some.

I invite you to notice over the next few days how many times you intervene and stop your children from exploring. Observe each situation and decide whether to react, and how to react. Can you hold back your fears?

Instilling independence

It is not what you do for your children, but what you have taught them to do for themselves, that will make them a successful human being—Ann Landers

Most parents want their children to be independent, and we can sow the seeds of emotional, physical and cognitive independence. What is important to understand is that *everything independent* starts as *dependent*. A climate of fulfilling a child's emotional needs provides a safe and secure foundation for them to grow independence. Only when their emotional needs are fulfilled can children move on to 'the next stage' through trial and error. We want to create a positive spiral of self-belief and capability.

When observing independent children, I see parents who do not jump in to do things for them. They hold back their reaction until – and only if – a child asks them to, or displays frustration. When your baby tries to discover what the purpose of a spoon is, just watch her, let her play with it – you don't need to provide any answers. When your toddler is trying to figure out how to build a structure with building blocks, let him explore and find his own way. When your ten-year-old is trying to re-build an old radio, let her experiment and learn by trial and error.

You can observe, but do less than you might be inclined to, and they will become more independent.

It's okay to fail

Today's parents are, in many cases, over-protective of their children. They don't want to see their children feel bad about anything and try to protect them from negative emotions. But when children do not have the resources to cope with failure or negative emotions, they cannot really experience feeling good or capable.

For example, Anna picked up Leo, her seven-year-old son, from a football match. He looked devastated, saying that his team had lost the game. Anna saw his reaction and couldn't prevent herself from saying 'But I saw you scored a goal! You did really well, you should be very proud'. Leo said, 'But we lost. I don't want to go to football anymore.' Anna, trying her best to cheer him up, said, 'Next time you might win! Sometimes you win and sometimes you lose. You love football. Don't worry about it'. Leo became quiet, feeling she didn't understand him so there was no point in continuing.

After learning about the effects of protecting children from negative feelings, Anna wanted to try a different tactic. It wasn't long before she had a chance to practise it. Two weeks after this incident, she picked Leo up from a birthday party. He was sad that he hadn't won the dancing competition. This is how the conversation went:

Parent: 'Hmmm, it looks like you really wanted to win this competition.'

Leo: 'Yes, I danced really well, and the prize was a huge chocolate egg.'

Parent *(realising that in the past she would probably have said 'Well, I'll buy you a chocolate egg!' to try to protect him from the discomfort of his disappointment)*: 'You feel you did your best and you really wanted that chocolate!'

Leo (quiet for a couple of seconds): 'Yes. But you know it's only chocolate. The rest of the party was great fun!'

The conclusion is that failure in itself is *not* a negative thing. Your job as a parent is *not* to protect your child from negative experiences. Your job is to support and encourage your child so they feel connected and brave enough to take on the challenge of trying again – to become *resilient*.

By doing this, you increase their chances of success, and of feeling good when they do achieve their goals! In other words, your job is to support their engagement in the *process*, rather than encourage a particular result.

A climate of honesty

Do you believe that there's a climate of trust and honesty in your family? Most parents immediately answer 'Yes' to this question, but I ask you: is that really so?

How about the situations that I often hear parents discuss. Their child asks about 'the noises' emanating from their bedroom at night, and they say 'We were moving the furniture' or 'What noise? Maybe it was a dream'. When their child comments on their emotional state, asking 'Why are you sad mummy/ daddy?' and they reply 'It's nothing' or 'I've been peeling onions' or 'I'm not sad' (even when they are experiencing genuine sadness).

Not to mention when parents manipulate an answer because they are afraid that an honest one will cause conflict. And the most common question of all 'How do babies come to the world?' often still gets the answer 'The stork brings them'.

You might say it's an age-appropriate thing, but I believe we can be honest with children of every age, although the information they get will be different. In the examples above, here are some options:

'Mummy and daddy made love. I'm sorry it woke you up.'

'I'm sad because Uncle Alex is not feeling well. But don't worry about me – I can take care of myself.'

'I'm upset because I had a row with a colleague at work. But this is an adult thing and I can take care of myself so don't worry.'

As for the last question, about where babies come from, some parents get embarrassed, but you can say:

'That's a great question. We have a really good book that explains all about it. Let's read it together.'

I recommend *How Did I Begin?* by Mick Manning and Brita Granstrom. Using a book targeted at the child's age group to explain subjects you find challenging can work well. With regards to age-appropriateness – there is no age I would describe what positions we get into when we make babies!

As with every subject, knowing what and how much to tell is key, but in all cases you can be both honest and truthful.

Encouragement

Encouragement is defined as 'the action of giving someone support, confidence, or hope'. In other words, it is anything you say or do that increases another person's self-worth. By encouraging a child, we strengthen their courage and trust in themselves and others. It doesn't mean telling them what to do or how to do it. So when a child tries to dress themselves and finds it challenging, you can encourage them by pointing out their courage for trying in the first place:

'I really appreciate you trying to do it all by yourself.'

And by understanding their position:

'It's tricky to dress yourself, especially getting your arms through the sleeves! You're almost there!'

Or by offering sympathy and gentle tips:

'I remember how tricky it was for me to get dressed when I was young! What helped me was to put the front of the top face down on the floor and start with my head. See what tricks help you and let me know'.

Sometimes the encouragement comes long after the event. I remember when my five-year-old daughter was invited to the birthday party of a boy who didn't go to the same school as her. Her excitement changed when she got there and realised she didn't know any of the thirty children who were there. I stayed at the party, and she came to me from time to time for some security and encouragement. There was an entertainer who asked them to pair up with a partner, and she came back to me, looking puzzled. I said something like:

'It's tricky to find a partner when you don't know any of the other children.'

She looked around and found another 'puzzled-looking' girl and she joined up with her. This dance, between finding her place in a new group and coming to me for security, was perfectly understandable. The following night my husband and I were invited to a big party. While dancing together, he offered to bring some drinks, which I was happy about. But when he left I found myself dancing by myself surrounded by fifty people I didn't know! I immediately thought about my daughter's experience the previous day. The next morning I shared my experience with her, telling her that thinking about her courage helped me in my situation, and that, like her, I looked for someone else who was puzzled like me, and we danced together. As I said before, children love to hear about their parents' experiences. These small moments of shared experience (age-appropriate of course) provide a great source of encouragement, but encouragement can also consist of an empathic smile, a hug or a high-five. Find your own way to encourage your child – as long as it is in line with the definition: the action of giving someone support, confidence, or hope.

Am I spoiling my child?

One of the most common questions I hear is 'Am I spoiling my child?'. If you do something for your child that they already know how to do, or need to know by their age, then yes, you are spoiling them.

But spoiling is not all negative. I can make myself a coffee, but I love it when my husband makes one for me. I know how to cook, but I love it when someone else takes care of it for me. We can and *should* spoil sometimes, but when spoiling is a dominant *characteristic* of a relationship and is accompanied by over-protectiveness, it limits the development of independence.

Finding the balance with your children means being an authoritative parent. Authoritative parents are described thus on *Wikipedia*:

They "often help their children to find appropriate outlets to solve problems."

They "encourage children to be independent but still place limits on their actions."

They "are not usually as controlling as authoritarian parents, allowing the child to explore more freely, thus having them make their own decisions based upon their own reasoning."

They "set clear standards for their children, monitor the limits that they set, and also allow children to develop autonomy."

They "expect mature, independent, and age-appropriate behaviour of children."

"As a result, children of authoritative parents are more likely to be independent and self-reliant ... successful, well liked by those around them, generous and capable of self-determination."

When we limit children's independence by not providing opportunities (that is, by doing for them what they should do for themselves), we increase their sense of *frailty* when facing a challenge. They start to lose faith in their abilities at home and school. Remember what I said about sleeping with your child in the introduction to *Part One*? Well continuous experiences of this type will encourage an unhelpful dependence on the adults around them.

Your task for this week is to make a list of all the things you believe your children should be able to do for themselves. Prioritise each item on the list and start encouraging them to do it.

Constructive criticism is still criticism

One of my weaknesses is my tendency to criticise others – and myself. For many years I believed that I provided *constructive* criticism but, frankly, I know that criticism remains criticism, no matter what words I attach to it. It took me a long time to realise that I can do my children a favour by keeping my criticisms to myself – or getting rid of them altogether! What's the secret?

There's a book called *How To Talk So Children Will Listen*, in which the authors Adele Faber and Elaine Mazlish helpfully suggest giving information or understanding instead of criticism (*You needed to say ... You should have done ...*).

An example of giving *information* is when your child interrupts while you are working. You can say:

> 'I need to concentrate when I work. When you talk to me, it interrupts my thinking and that means it will take me longer to finish my work. I don't like it.'

And an example of being *understanding* is when your child tells you something upsetting that happened to her with a friend:

> 'I understand how this made you upset.'

In my experience, and the experiences of many parents I work with, is that providing children with information and understanding – as opposed to criticism – is the fastest way for them to learn and take on responsibilities.

It's hard enough to be children these days, and on the whole they neither need nor benefit from adults' criticisms. We want them to develop a positive self-image, and criticism hinders that.

- 8 -

The downside of praise

So what should we say when children complete a task – say, math problems – quickly and perfectly? Should we deny them the praise they have earned? Yes. When this happens, I say, "Whoops. I guess that was too easy. I apologize for wasting your time. Let's do something you can really learn from!"

Carol S. Dweck

Here I will explore the most effective ways to use praise, as well as its potential pitfalls.

The downside of praise

Sometimes the areas in which we praise our children the most are where our greatest expectations are hiding. These days, parents tend to over-praise their children, possibly as a result of the competitive culture we live in – as a way to soften the pressure. But not all children react the same way to praise. Some find it encouraging, while others see it as an 'expectation' for the next time – they may think it's too risky to try again. In the same way you would probably quite like to quit after getting exceptional feedback from your boss, rather than risk failing to meet expectations again.

Your child may feel pressure like this from being praised – their reaction to praise will tell you about their confidence. Here's the tip:

> Try to reduce praise for results with comments like 'Wow! Amazing drawing' and 'Well done for getting ten out of ten on the test' and appreciate the process they went through instead, by reflecting on their determination, their courage to try, their patience, and their motivation.

When you describe what you see without judgement, you encourage the child to keep going. For example:

> 'You drew all these little details with lots of patience.'
>
> 'I saw how hard you studied for that exam.'
>
> 'I really like it when you try new types of food.'

The "I worked hard!" way

Once a day or once a week, maybe at the end of the day, celebrate hard work by playing this game with your child. It goes like this:

> Parent: 'I worked hard today/this week for —' *(something you feel proud of yourself for)*
>
> Parent and child *(loudly and with great energy)*: 'Well done, mummy/ daddy, well done!' *(give energetic congratulations and hugs)*
>
> Child: 'I worked hard today/this week for —' *(whatever they are proud of)*
>
> Parent and child *(loudly and with great energy)*: 'Well done, Ethan! Well done!' *(energetic congratulations and hugs)*

Here, the emphasis is on the *effort*, not the accomplishment. For example, I can be proud of working hard to be on time, working hard to understand a problem at work, working hard to concentrate on a task, or working hard to make sure I have time for myself. You will notice the first couple of times you do this, your children will imitate you. But with practise and time, they will bring their own ideas and achievements.

What I especially like about this game is that, when it's part of the family routine, we all look for positive things during the day to mention later, which means we increase our awareness for appreciation. It's also a great way to encourage effort, rather than results. It acknowledges that your child might work really hard during a tennis game and still lose.

Celebrating their effort and hard work builds a positive self-image and encourages them to work harder. Another great way to end a day!

Find the pride inside

If you're keen to reduce your children's need for your approval, teach them how to locate their 'inner pride'. When they do something and run to you for approval, wait with the 'Well done!' and instead reflect on their achievement:

> 'You jumped from the third step!'

Then ask them how it made them feel. If your child is too young to express how they feel, or seems overwhelmed by the question, you can add:

> 'I bet you're very proud of yourself!'

It's really that simple!

Encouragement versus praise

Encouragement, which was discussed in Chapter 6, differs from *praise* in that it can be given *regardless* of the outcome and allows children to develop pride in themselves, rather than depending on praise from their parents. Encouragement fosters a positive self-image, which in turn allows them to continue to improve and grow in confidence as they develop better and better skills. Negative feedback can easily discourage them, but positivity *always* delivers results.

Praise based on results sounds like:

'Well done, you put the top on the right way.'

Encouragement sounds like:

'It's tricky to get dressed on your own. I like it when you try to do it by yourself.'

Praise based on results sounds like:

'Wow! This is the best school report you've had!'

Or for a less good report:

'Maybe next time you need to study harder so that you will have good results.'

Encouragement sounds like:

'I bet you feel proud receiving such a report after you worked so hard this term' or (for a less good report) 'You studied very hard this term. It can be very disappointing not to have the result you wanted.'

Delete the brackets

When I present couples with an 'appreciation exercise', they think it's easy. They say things like '*I really appreciate that you weren't angry yesterday*' or '*I appreciate that you didn't put pressure on me yesterday to be at home on time*' or '*I appreciate you didn't criticise my sister yesterday like you've done before*'.

However, this is not *positive* appreciation. Appreciation should be totally positive, without any mention of 'no' or 'not' or any comparison to a previous experience. The same is true with children. The examples below show (in brackets) which part should be deleted:

'You really helped me this morning by being ready on time and doing everything all by yourself (*without fighting with me*).'

'It's nice to see how you cared for your sister today (*not hitting her like you did yesterday*).'

Appreciation should be clean and positive.

Mindsets for growth

A *growth* mindset is seen in people who believe their abilities can grow, who think it doesn't matter who you are, you can get smarter. Working really hard makes them feel good and capable of improving. Their inner voice says 'If it gets harder, I can work harder/come up with a strategy or focus more'. A *fixed* mindset is seen in people who believe they have only a limited amount of a quality and 'that's it', so their inner voice says 'I'm not intelligent/not so smart and I cannot change it'. The question is, how do we orient our children to the growth mindset?

Dr Carol Dweck is a leading researcher of the growth mindset. In a series of famous studies she presented children aged nine or ten with four sets of puzzles. The first set was easy, and at the end of the task, the 'instructor' praised the children:

- The first group was told 'You did really well! You must be really smart' and the second group was told 'You did really well! You must try really hard'.

Then the children were given a second set of puzzles, which were much harder and they might struggle with. The idea was to see what happened to their confidence and motivation and whether there was any difference between the groups getting different words of praise.

- The first group (praised for intelligence) generally thought they were not smart or not good at the second task – a very discouraging belief relating to a fixed mindset. The second group (praised for effort) saw the second set of puzzles as an opportunity to learn from the challenge – a growth mindset.

Then there was a third task. The children were allowed to choose whether they wanted another easy set of puzzles or more challenging ones.

- Among the first group (praised for intelligence) a third chose the tough task, but two-thirds didn't want to risk losing their 'smart' label. Among the second group (praised for effort) nine tenths chose the tough task. They wanted to prove just how hard working they were.

Then, the experiment came full circle. The children were given the chance to do yet another task, as easy as the first one.

- The first group (praised for intelligence) performed less well (20% worse) than they did in the first easy task, even though it was no harder. The second group (praised for effort) were 30% better. Their failure in the more challenging tasks had actually spurred them on.

All these differences between the two groups of children were brought about by *six simple words* spoken after the first test. As Dweck concluded: *'Praising children's intelligence harms motivation and it harms performance'*. What can we take from this?

- Children need to experience the process of making mistakes *and failing*, then bouncing back and recovering. As they grow, they'll be much better at facing challenges.
- Children are sensitive to our judgements and values. All praise words sound like confidence-boosters, but *they are not*!
- We should teach children to see challenges as learning opportunities rather than threats, so they see them as an opportunity and a place they can learn from.

Their achievement or yours?

Sometimes I hear parents express great excitement over their child's achievement but it can be difficult to distinguish whose feelings they are!

A parent excitedly said to me in front of her child 'You wouldn't believe what a great school report he brought to me. I was so proud that it made my day. I was in heaven'.

Another told me he said to his son, after watching his school concert 'Wow, what a great guitar performance. It was amazing. After I worked so hard with you, I can see the results. You made me very happy today'.

What's wrong with these words?

They emphasises the parent's effort or feelings of accomplishment – not the child's. I remind parents like this that it's their child's report, their child's concert – their child's achievement. I remind them to ask the child how they feel about their achievement, and pay less attention to the result; this will avoid discouraging them, increasing their dependency, and reducing their self-confidence. No-one wants children to need us as the source of approval for everything – we want them to have it within themselves and to follow their own directions.

The next time you are over-excited about something your child has done, remember that you don't want it to become your moment, or about your feelings. It is your child's moment to shine and you shouldn't take that away from them. How can you tell when you aren't doing it right? Because your sentences will be about you and your feelings. Your excitement will exceed your children's. Your focus will be on how hard you worked for them to achieve this. You will not be asking your children about their feelings.

Finally, make sure that your pleasure doesn't swamp theirs. The excitement should be theirs – it isn't all about us.

Abilities are developed

When a child tries to master a new skill, it's very easy to take on the belief 'I can't do it!' Helping children understand that their abilities *can* be developed and transformed is important. There are several ways to do this. You can talk about the progress they made from a previous time:

> 'Do you remember how tricky it was for you to find the right shoe for each foot? Now you know how to do that! Now think about the direction you need to close the shoe strap.'

You can also mention your own process of mastering a particular skill. Another idea is something I've heard in some schools, where they have a no 'fail' result in tests; instead they have a 'not yet' result, which means the child is in the *process* of learning – allowing growth without the label of failure, emphasising the development and belief in the transformation of abilities. In one of my daughter's schools, a particular teacher banned the words 'I can't'. The children were not allowed to say it. She offered them an alternative: 'I practise and practise and practise until I can do it'. When my daughter asked my husband something, he said 'I can't' (because he was busy) and she responded 'You're not allowed to say those words'.

Don't say it if you don't believe it!

Rachel came to see me about her teenage daughter, Claire. Rachel wanted to improve her relationship with Claire and was finding it difficult. There was a lack of trust, and she felt there was nothing she hadn't tried. She said she used positive language and praise, even in challenging situations. Now, Claire loved to sing. She sang a lot and had a strong voice, but Rachel thought her singing was awful – out of tune, too loud, like 'one long scream'. Rachel didn't want to hurt Claire's feelings, but found the singing hard to endure for hour after hour at home. So she told Claire: 'You have a lovely voice, and it's wonderful that you like to sing, but can you sing in your room because your baby brother is sleeping now and it's too much'.

She wanted to strengthen feelings of trust and honesty, but by saying that she didn't express her need and projected it onto the brother; this will only increase sibling rivalry. How could Rachel praise Claire's practising of singing, and also take into account Rachel's needs – to be honest without upsetting Claire? You might recall that the best praise is observation – without opinion or judgment – but you can include your needs. So it could be something like this:

> 'I see you love to practise your singing, which is wonderful. When I'm at home I sometimes need quiet and space. Do you think you can practise in your room today?'

What you say is not what they hear

Parents believe that when they say to their child 'You are clever' or 'You are beautiful' or 'You are honest' and so on, that they're building their self-confidence. Unfortunately, this couldn't be further from the truth. Children and adults hear things differently.

Tomas, a father of two, once told me he didn't understand why his son didn't feel clever. He thought his son was very clever and he told him so – a lot. I asked Tomas whether his parents thought he had been clever as a child to which he replied 'Yes, they told me all the time'. Then I asked 'And when they did that, did you feel clever?'. He said, blushing 'Actually, no. I still don't think I'm clever'. Here was a very wise and capable man who didn't believe he was clever, even though his parents made sure they told him how clever he was.

What's the problem here? The problem is that when a parent says *'You're clever'*, the child thinks *'I'm stupid'*.

This might sound surprising, but when children hear words like this they automatically think about all the reasons they do not feel or experience that they were clever.

The trick is not to praise a personality trait, but to describe a specific situation. You want your children to hear what you say – and translate it in their minds into praise. Take the following example:

'Oh wow! That was a difficult quiz and I see you finished it!'

From words like this, children can conclude 'If it was challenging and I did it, it probably means I am capable!'.

Roz, a mother of three, used this suggestion with her middle son, who was extremely shy, when he sang a song at a karaoke party. She told him afterwards:

'Wow! It takes lots of courage to go up on stage and sing. I really enjoyed your voice'.

Can you see the difference between this statement and one like: 'Your song was the best!'?

Praise patience

Another scenario. You're queueing at a supermarket checkout and your child gets fidgety and starts complaining and wants to go home. You respond calmly several times, but he gets more demanding and louder. What do you say? What do you do? In the past, when children were not at the centre of the family, they developed patience. In most cases, they knew they had to wait for attention, for their turn in a game or in a queue. Now, they are at the centre of the family, with parents who are often so concerned about their feelings that they fulfil any request instantly. These are the sort of things I've seen:

- Two parents talking outside the school: the child comes up, stands between them, tries to say something, and his parent stops the conversation to answer immediately.
- A parent having a coffee break or talking on the phone: the child interrupts them with a request and they stop talking and do as requested.
- A child asks for water: the parent runs to get some.
- A child not wanting to eat: the family sits down to eat and he doesn't join them.
- A child not wanting to wait for her birthday to get something she wants: her parents go and buy it for her rather than make her wait.

Parents are now so concerned about their children's feelings of frustration that they act well before there's any sign of negative feelings. By doing this, they are *training* their children not to be patient! Having patience is a crucial part of childhood and adulthood, so what positive steps can you take here? Simply notice when and where your child shows patience and say something about it:

'You waited very patiently for your turn in the game.'

'Thank you for waiting with your homework question until I finished my bath.'

'Ah! Here's the waitress with your food. You have a lot of patience waiting for that! I'm really impressed.'

When this is what you notice, this is what's going to grow in your child. Now back to the supermarket checkout. There are many options for how to react. One is to comment on what you want – not only what you see. You might see that your child loses patience, but until that point he had done his best. So say something like:

'You have a lot of patience. You helped me with all the shopping, and waited with me here for so long! What a lot of patience! We still have another two people in front of us, so do you want to play 'I spy with my little eye' in the meantime?'

Thus you praise what you want to have *more of*, and provide an alternative to their behaviour.

In place of praise or judgement

This is from the *Connected Parent, Thriving Children* programme developed by Harville Hendrix and Helen LaKelly Hunt:

'It is invaluable to learn and perfect neutral observation – mirroring – in place of praise or evaluation of any kind. This is a reflection of what you see your child doing or hear them saying. We want to notice, and to let the children know we are attuned to them. Praising can diminish the supportive effects of mirroring. If we tell the child she is doing a "great job", or that he is "a good boy", we risk setting them up for expecting praise and learning to seek that in place of following their own inner direction. It also sets up the perception of being "bad", or doing a "bad job", when a child isn't meeting the expectations a parent has set.

'I remember speaking about how to praise in one of my parenting classes. To put their learning into practise, I asked each parent to create whatever they wanted from some basic arts and crafts materials. Each parent had to say something about the art of the parent next to them, describing what they saw and how it made them feel (based on the principle of eliminating judgement and criticism). One parent said to the parent next to her: "I'm happy to practise with you, as your design is the most creative. The way you work with the blue and red material is very creative and the shape makes me smile".'

What do you think about that? It sounded like it met the criteria, but something didn't feel right to me. After a moment I understood. Read the first statement again. Although it was positive, it involved *judgement* – the word 'most', a comparison. And when we compare, we judge.

Here is a simple alternative that is clean and encouraging:

'I can see the creative thinking behind your work. The way you used the blue and red … '

- 9 -
Beyond play:
Creating confidence

Enjoy the little things, for one day you may look back and realize
they were the big things.
Robert Brault

In this chapter you will find tips on how to develop a child's confidence, independence and well-being through play and everyday tasks.

Free time is golden

With our over-pressured culture, children 'need' to learn how to read, write, play an instrument, swim, ride a bike, and excel in ballet and football all by the age of five! Their 'free time' is over-scheduled. You need to make sure your child has *enough time to be a child*. Give them plenty of time and encouragement for imaginary, independent play or free play with their brothers, sisters, cousins and friends. It really helps children to learn and develop.

In my opinion, children do not need afterschool clubs before the age of 6, and thereafter I recommend no more than two afterschool clubs in a week. Free time is *golden*.

Create space

I woke up one morning and realised just how many toys we had in the house. Then I started asking parents at workshops how many toys they have. Even counting similar toys as one (one box of dressing up clothes, one box of building blocks, etc.), the average was eighty! It's like the number of friends people have on Facebook! However, those with two hundred friends are only in weekly contact with about eight of them. The same is true for toys. Children need just a few – three or four – *quality* toys for their entertainment and development. Things like building blocks, arts and crafts materials, puzzles and pretending games. Although it might seem counter-intuitive, children *play more* when they have *less* toys!!

Every now and again, have a toy clear-out: give them away, sell them, place them in storage for younger children – just make more space and time for play.

Take a step back

You watch your daughter from a close distance in the playground, climbing really well up a rope, but she stops at the highest level. She calls you 'Mum, help me. I'm stuck.' What's your instinct? What do you do? Do you rush to rescue her? If this happens, go to her – but wait before giving advice. Talk about her achievement so far and ask her what she thinks she can do to reach the top.

> 'Hey! You climbed so high! You have lots of courage. How do you think you can climb to the top from there?'

Your presence and encouragement will most likely spur her to go on. And the bonus is that when she starts nursery or school, she will already have the inner confidence to solve her own problems!

The benefits of boredom

Children who know how to be 'bored' have a brilliant ability to transform something with no significance into something amazing, to relax themselves after a busy day, to find a new area for learning and enjoyment, or to wait patiently for something more exciting. Genius comes from boring moments! If you, the parents. don't allow yourself moments of calmness and relaxed joyfulness, you will find it challenging to provide moments like that to your children. Let your children have enough time to do nothing. They are developing their minds and motivations. As Tiger Woods (one of the most successful golfers of all times) once said:

> 'Don't force your children into sports. I never was. To this day, my dad has never asked me to go play golf. I ask him. It's the child's desire to play that matters, not the parent's desire to have the child play. Fun. Keep it fun.'

Playing equals learning

You have a lifetime to work, but children are only young once.—*Polish proverb*

For children under the age of six, playing *is* learning. Sadly, advertisers play on your anxiety by stressing how crucial their products toys and learning aids are to children's development. You are told that your children should be reading and writing at an early age, or that they well be more intelligent if they listen or watch DVDs containing classical music. However, this is far from true. It's actually the opposite! This educational approach places undue pressure on parents *and* children, creating anxiety and stress all round. So keep the stress out of your relationships! Play with your children, and let them play by themselves – it truly is the most effective and productive way for them to learn.

Be where you are

*To be in your children's memories tomorrow, you have to be in their lives today—**Unknown source***

You're at work, thinking about your child, wishing you could be with him or her. You're with your child, thinking about what to make for dinner. You're making dinner, thinking about an erotic night with your partner. You're in bed with your partner, having sex, and thinking about work!! Do you get the picture? Whatever you do – be *present*!

Bring play to chores

Parents are always busy with all the 'stuff' that needs to be done at home. But did you know that your children would be delighted to help out? You just need to change the way they see tasks – not as chores but opportunities to play. They also allow you to strengthen the bonds with your children. So if the toys need tidying up, try these games:

> Put a song onto play and play the game of 'putting everything in place before it ends'.
>
> Name a colour, and see who can put the most things of that colour back in their place.
>
> Write down numbers on pieces of paper and put them face down. Pick one up, and that's the number of toys to put in their place. This is great for children who are learning numbers.

This might require some PR on your behalf to *market* boring work as something exciting, but these things need to be done, and this can be a superb option.

Be the base

*If you have never been hated by your child, you have never been a parent—**Bette Davis***

These days, parents want to be their children's best friend. But our job is to say 'No' to the most enjoyable things they want to do: picking their noses, touching their poo, touching their intimate parts in front of others, sucking their thumbs, playing with dirt, making lots of noise, or just relaxing and unwinding! You want to be their friend, but they do not need more friends. They need *available* and *reliable* parents. So act like one! Whether you want to avoid conflict, or feel guilty for not being present in your children's lives, or believe it's not your job, it's not in your best interests to *not* guide your children about appropriate ways of behaving. Instead, lead your family to a 'safe base' by setting healthy boundaries and being the adult in the relationship.

"Stop" and "Go"

Do you find it difficult when you're out and about with your children and they run away and don't listen when you call them to stop? You can teach them how to listen to your instructions by practising this as a game, next time you are out in a safe place with them:

Tell them that when you say 'Run!' they need to run. When you say 'Stop!' they need to stop.

Start by saying 'Run!' or 'Go!', then say 'Stop!' after a five-second gap.

Then try to confuse them by saying 'Run! Stop!' in the same second, or 'Run! Run!' or 'Stop! Stop!' to see if they react to what they expect or actually hear.

Have fun by reversing roles sometimes, so that they get to give the instructions.

Children love this game and it's a great opportunity to get the message across that when you say 'Stop!' you expect them to stop. If you play this game enough, it becomes an automatic response.

Build a happy playground

While we try to teach our children all about life, our children teach us what life is all about—Angela Schwindt

One of the most important tips I can give for better parenting is to be a *better partner*. Your 'couple relationship' is the playground in which your children are growing. When the emotional climate of your family is positive and healthy, it creates a solid sense of safety and promotes a confident way of being.

Cherish and thrive in your couple relationship. Make enough time and space among the day-to-day routine to have fun with your partner, and to build and strengthen your relationship. Ask yourself:

• When was the last time you had fun together?

• When was the last time you surprised each other?

• When was the last time you enjoyed an intimate connection with each other?

• When was the last time you had lunch together without children?

• When was the last time you shared an adventure together?

Bring the spark back to your relationship, if not for yourself, then for your children.

Putting it all together

Positive parenting is about being an effective *educator*. It's about understanding and believing that the actions you take with your children *today* will create the adults they'll become.

Positive parents know that in every communication (or lack of) there is a message for their children. These can be negative messages about themselves (*I can't go to sleep by myself, therefore I'm not capable … I'm not listening, therefore I'm a bad person*), or about you (*Mum's unfair … Dad doesn't care … I can't tell my parents how I feel*), or about being in a relationship (*relationships are painful*), but you can use their early, valuable years to teach them positive messages about liking who they are, about feeling connected to you, and about a healthy couple relationship.

Being a positive and connected parent provides the foundation for everything you wish to experience with and for your children. When you speak in a positive way, your children feel positive and connected, and so they act in a positive way with you and others. Using positive words creates a positive self-image for them, and when they feel good about themselves they are more like to cooperate, to express how they feel in words (rather than acting out with behaviour), and to be kind to others.

It is challenging for parents who are raised amid negativity, and it is challenging when your children challenge you – but it is within your control. The effect of what you do will spread like a stone creating ripples in water. By thinking creatively about what and how you communicate with your child, you will find many alternatives to the words '*No*' … '*Not*' … '*Why*' … '*But*'.

Many parents say that what made them want to make changes was realising how often they said these negative words! It's a good starting point. I suggest coming up with three other ways to communicate messages in a positive way – and write them down!

The more you think about and practise them, the more accessible they will be in times of need.

Yet it's inevitable that you will experience some challenges when it comes to raising children.

Part Two of this book addresses exactly that.

PART TWO

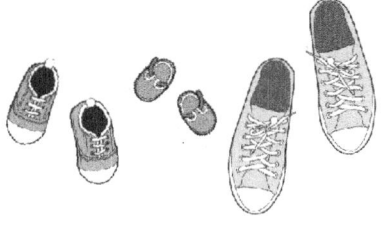

SMALL STEPS TO

Turning Challenges
into
Opportunities

REACTION VERSUS
CONSCIOUS CONNECTION

Introduction to Part Two

Having tried some of the tips in the earlier chapter, you may have noticed a difference in the atmosphere at home. You may also have experienced improvements in your children's behaviour during the day. But it's inevitable that you'll come up against major challenges. Parents face tantrums, sadness, difficult boundary-setting and difficult-to-please children. Children can lie, say 'No' to everything, refuse to go to sleep, and challenge your authority. However, they are doing exactly what is *normal* at different stages in their psychological development, and such challenges are *necessary* for their growth *and* your own!

Now you will learn to 're-image' your children as young people simply acting for their own development – not against you! You will find out how to avoid escalating situations, how to react consciously, and connect in a way that will help your child self-regulate their feelings, and help you set boundaries in a calm and healthy way. At Imago, we believe that many (if not all) cases of misbehaviour arise when children feel disconnected to their significant caregiver. They act out some longing or need –the need to feel loved, to feel capable, or for boundaries and differentiation (I'm not you and that's okay) – which can be viewed as misbehaving. Usually they are longing for connection. Maintaining connection during conflicting situations is vital for helping them overcome challenges, to self-regulate their emotions, to let go and to move on.

Whatever the challenge is, you can increase your understanding of what your children are trying to tell you through their behaviour – and why it is so triggering for you. This will help you transform any challenge into an opportunity for connection and growth, to move from being reactive to your child's behaviour to being consciously connected.

Looking back is the first step forward

Nobody can go back and start a new beginning, but anyone can start today and make a new ending—Maria Robinson

We all bring our own baggage to parenthood. By baggage, I mean what comes from the specific family culture we were raised in. We were all raised in a unique family culture in which some emotions were more tolerated than others. In some families, showing anger was *not* an option (*You're not really upset … There's nothing to be upset about*). In other families, showing vulnerability was interpreted as a weakness and level of neediness that was not appreciated or tolerated (*You cry like a baby … Come on, you're a big boy … Big boys don't cry*). In others, being smart or opinionated was treated in shaming ways (*You think you're so smart, don't you?*). Which feelings were not accepted in *your* family?

Intrusion vs neglect parenting

We may also have had parents who, when responding to our feelings, were either too intrusive or were neglectful. Intrusive parents are those who are over-involved, who smother, mind-read and have invasive behaviours. They may have reacted over-emotionally, becoming upset or hysterical as a result of your behaviour, leading to punishments, blame, criticism or shaming.

At the other end of the scale are *neglectful* parents. They tend to be under-involved, detached, disinterested and they avoid connection. They may send their children away and minimise their children's feelings (*I'll give you something to cry about … You don't have any reason to be upset … Not now – I'm busy*), and become depressed and so on. Intrusive or neglectful parenting behaviours can take place to varying degrees in different families, yet none of these approaches creates safety for – or increases connection with – the child.

Just how many of us were raised by adults who were present, connected and helpful when we were upset, angry or afraid? How many of us have had the benefit of a 'model' parent or adult to show us how to consciously react to a child with challenging behaviour?

So, as children, we may have experienced hurt and pain as a consequence of our parents' behaviour. And as a result, we often develop defence mechanisms against their ineffective parenting. For more on this, see *Giving The Love That Heals* by Harville Hendrix and Helen LaKelly Hunt. We may have lost touch with any of our emotions that were downplayed or forbidden – or we may deny that they exist. Some of us feel negatively about how we were parented, yet find ourselves acting in similar ways.

Our own children's 'issues' or 'problems' often touch on our personal history – our baggage – and challenge various defence mechanisms we may have developed. For example, a parent who as a child was praised for doing things by himself by an under-involved parent might have an adult defence mechanism that manifests as a need for space and independence. Having a child who is 'clingy' or 'needy' might challenge that way of being. The parenting model that these parents bring to the present is not about connection, so a new way to connect when they feel challenged is necessary not only for their children, but for their own growth and development as well.

Saying that, maintaining a connection with our children when we are triggered, tired, anxious or stressed is a skill that can take a lifetime to master.

The perfection gap: fantasy meets reality

While growing up, we may have fantasised about the perfect parents we would be. We may have dreamed about being like the parents from a happy movie we saw, or like our friends' 'cool' parents, or other relatives we adored. We picked up all the positive things we wanted to pass on, and many of us swore that we would *never* be like our own parents. But most of us also had the fantasy and expectation that our children would be kind, considerate, able to play by themselves, good at sharing and patient, capable of regulating their emotions (even though they wouldn't need to do so, because their life would be so happy with us as their parents!). Their teachers would love them. They would be independent – and a pleasure to be with. Life would be all sweetness and honey!

Then we become parents. We experience the weight of responsibility, the infinite and repetitive day-to-day tasks of caring for our children and running a household while working. We may experience a sense of being underappreciated and taken for granted, and worn out by the endless 'fire-fighting' involved.

There is usually a huge gap between the fantasy and the reality. It is in this context that our children evoke some of our deepest family-of-origin issues. Their behaviours can be especially challenging when they contrast with our own family culture. If, as an adult, you show no anger because you learned that anger is not acceptable (and possibly shut down the feeling of being angry altogether) you may be particularly challenged by an angry child, who doesn't mind expressing it loud and clear! If you were shamed for being sensitive, you might find it difficult to deal with a sensitive, vulnerable child. If exploring the world around you was not permitted by an anxious, over-involved parent, you might be challenged by your child's exploration at a stage where their developmental task is to explore the world around them.

The root of your challenge

Taking it all together, when you find yourself being especially challenged by a specific behaviour (whether it's neediness, crying, stubbornness, sensitivity, loudness or controlling tactics) it might be because:

• You've lost, repressed or shut down a feeling or behaviour, because from early on you understood it was not acceptable and spent many years (un-consciously) hiding it, so it is no longer in your awareness. If you now find yourself with a very demanding, loud, and challenging child, it might be because you were not allowed a 'voice' in your own family.

• You have a particular feeling or behaviour, and express it – but you hate it. You are aware of it and you consciously want to overcome it. For example, you may be over-critical of your children, and see how damaging it is, but don't know how to stop it.

• You have a feeling or behaviour that you express, but it is not in your awareness. In other words, you deny it. It relates to all the things that your friends and family (especially your partner) tell you about yourself, to which you say 'That's not true. I don't act like that!'

The point is that many parents react to their children without knowing they bring their own baggage to the present. They think it is all about the specific child and locate the problem in the child. And because of our unconscious sensitivities, we might react in a way that creates a negative spiral – not only escalating the situation, but creating disconnection that can generate even greater problems than the initial one. Through awareness of our selves, our children, and the relationship between us, we can choose to react with *intention* in challenging situations.

Part Two of this book will help you transform any challenge into an opportunity for connection and growth, to move from being reactive to your child's behaviour to being consciously and intentionally connected. You may experience challenges which, while they might not seem so at the time, can be the best things that happen to your family. It's often because a problem presents itself that parents start to think about what's going on in their child's mind. The following chapters will help you understand what your child is trying to communicate to you through their behaviour, and what growth that challenge offers you. Among the many tips offered, you will find out how to react to a frustrated child, to tantrums and feelings of sadness, to deal with difficult-to-please children and how to set boundaries in a calm and healthy way. You will learn that by modelling your own capacity for flexible thinking, you can help develop your child's.

Practicing the tips and experiencing the results will increase your confidence in your parenting style, which will result in a more relaxed, and satisfying connection between you and your child. However (as I've said many times through this book), changing the way we parent when we are not in challenging situations is the key to success for coping with any issue that arises.

All the suggestions are based on extensive research and experience about improving parent–child relationships, but they do not attempt to replace the therapeutic process or parental consultations. If you find situations to be too challenging, please seek professional support.

- 10 -
Parenting visions for challenging times

The children who need the most love will ask for it in the most unloving of ways.
Unknown source

You can't teach children to behave better by making them feel worse. When children feel better, they behave better.
Pam Leo

It's easier to be a positive parent when everyone gets along, but how can you keep your values in mind when you're being challenged? The following tips are designed to help you turn your family vision into reality and bring more fun, joy and confidence to your parenting experience, by guiding you to react in a connected and intentional way to difficult situations with you children.

Walk the walk

Be great in act, as you have been in thought—William Shakespeare

You love your children, and this feeling is important. Very important. But *actions* are even more important! In many cases, it doesn't matter how you feel – what matters is what you do! Many parents tell me how much they love their children but find themselves screaming at them, 'losing it', getting angry with them. You may struggle to regulate your own feelings of anger and think that it doesn't matter if you often explode in front of your children – as long as they know you love them. Think again! As I said, it's not how you feel – it's how you act. When you scream at your children, they hate your scream, and at that moment they probably hate you. So everyone feels bad.

If you feel love, then take responsibly and act in loving ways. When you take all the negativity out of the equation, the real problem (if there is one) will be much clearer and easier to address. You're probably asking yourself 'How will I know if I've done it effectively?' Well, if you deal with a challenge and still feel good about yourself afterwards, that's a sure sign that you did it effectively.

Let your 'better part' speak and act lovingly towards your loved ones.

Build from a strong core

Write down answers to these questions, where the emphasis is on the word 'most':

- What is the *most* important thing about you as a person?
- What is the *most* important thing about you as a parent?

The latter is not always obvious, so keep asking yourself 'Why is that important to me?' until you identify the most important thing. The concepts here are inspired by the well-known therapists Pat Love and Steven Stosny who wrote *How to Improve Your Marriage Without Talking About It*. They talk about core values – you have identified your own by answering the questions above. They said:

> 'Every time you violate your core values – even if you are just reacting to your child – you feel guilty.'

Simply put, if your core value is to be a loving and calm parent and you lose it and shout at your child, then you will feel guilty. The *gap* between your values and actions creates guilt. You can maintain your core values and avoid this gap. One of the ways to keep doing this is to *slow down*. Breathe. Think.

For starters, think about whether the way you react in certain situations with your children is in-line with your core values. What do *you* think your child thinks is the most important thing about you as a parent or a person today? How can you bring your beliefs and core values to your actions and how can you implement them today?

Make the magic come alive

Make a list about how you would like your children to feel when they are around you. Do they actually feel that way around you? If yes, that's great! Continue doing what you are already doing. But if not, what can you do that will make your child feel that way in your presence? Today is the day to start doing it!

Whether you want your children to feel positive, relaxed, secure, safe, appreciated, loved or anything else, you can make it happen. It is one of the keys for a fulfilled relationship to make our children feel good about themselves when they're around us.

So, today, make a point of appreciating your children, reassure them, notice them, acknowledge their perspectives and needs, listen more than be heard, and relax – and see the magic happen!!

Own your lake

Do you know the story about the fisherman who always fished at the same corner of the same lake, using the same technique and the same bait – and caught the same fish all the time. He couldn't understand why. In this analogy, the fish are our partners and children. We find it easy to analyse them, but really it is about you – the fisherman.

Ask yourself: Are you trying to make changes in your children's behaviour? Are you doing it by criticising, shaming, blaming, punishing or just being negative towards them? I have yet to meet parents who, through punishment, blame and negativity raised an independent, confident and cooperative child. These kind of fishermen have to learn to change their location around the lake; to get some new fishing skills. In other words, take on their responsibilities.

Your task for this weekend is to try to let go of all negativity and focus on the positive things your close ones bring into your life. Tell your children how lucky you are to have them in your life. Use your resources (family, friends and community) to learn new skills and put them into practice – and find a different corner in your lake.

Wear rose-tinted glasses

You may find your children struggling with something that concerns you. Maybe you wish they had more friends? Or that they would be more responsible? Maybe you'd like them to be more open to new ideas or have more determination?

Try this:

> Close your eyes, take some deep breaths, and see your child in your imagination as you want them to be in twenty years time. Really imagine them successfully handling the concerns you envisaged above. These are your rose-tinted glasses.

> Open your eyes and see (imagine) your children like that now. When you look at them, speak with or react to them, put on your rose-tinted glasses and interact as if they have that quality! You want them to be more responsible? Give them small responsibilities, talk to them as someone who is responsible, and expect them to act responsibly.

You won't believe how much positive change you can create by changing the way you connect with your children in this way.

See struggle as a good thing

'What do you want to happen now?' I asked Angela, the mother of a six-year-old boy with challenging behaviour. 'I just want him to be happy,' she said in desperation. She further expressed that she was afraid of repeating her parents' mistakes and wanted an ideal and 'normal' family. She found it very challenging to contain her son's frustration, so she did everything she could to prevent it happening in the first place – even if that meant speaking on his behalf in conflicts with his friends, bringing his ball back in the park if he didn't want to fetch it, helping with his homework, getting him dressed, and more besides. This boy was *the centre* of the family. His needs and wants were more important than those of his parents or anyone around him. It was my job to tell her that if *his* happiness remained *her* focus, he was likely to become miserable, frustrated and bitter.

Some parents have the following attitude about their children: 'You don't need to make an effort – mummy/daddy are here to save you'. This is a dangerous message to give out. These parents behave like slaves and create a spoiled and unhappy child. Why? Because some level of frustration and effort are essential to child development. Healthy frustration and conflict resolution are the foundations for problem-solving, creativity, and a sense of pride. They are qualities that are now, and in the years to come, the basis of happy moments.

Parents must be able to physically or emotionally contain a frustrated child. What needs to be done is to slow down on the interventions. Wait. Observe. Give children an opportunity to find their own way to moments that they finds pleasurable and satisfying.

See the amazing!

Our brains are wired to notice negative stuff about ourselves, our partners and our children. But what do children need? Your children say:

> 'Look at me! See how amazing I am. Even if I wet the bed at night, or can't sleep easily, or find it challenging to control my anger or excel at school – look at me! I also have a positive side. Love me. Don't do things I can do myself. Give me the tools and skills to achieve them.'

See the amazing. And when you are challenged by your children, speak to the amazing! Then you can hold the positive images of them at a time when they least show it. We can help them to see themselves in a different and a positive way, which invites the possibility for acting appropriately. Speak to the amazing child.

Choose children – not screens

Screens on iPhones, TVs, computers, iPads ... These are the *cancer* of relationships. They quickly destroy healthy parts. Don't cooperate with the cancer. This analogy may seem extreme, but consider this: when someone is engaged with a screen, they are avoiding relationships. And there are consequences to avoiding connection.

There are record numbers of children and adults experiencing depression, more divorced and 'emotionally divorced' couples (they are still together but only as room-mates), and sex and intimacy between couples are at an all-time low!

So, be present with your loved ones. You can decide how long to be present for. With your children, it might be twenty minutes a day, an hour or two a day, or one day at the weekend. Whatever you choose, do it without interference from screen time. Turn off all screens and just be present. Think about the message your children get when you're playing with them and your phone rings. You don't pick up and they think you didn't hear it, and tell you someone called. And you answer:

'I can't take that call now. I'm busy with a very important person!'

It is in *your* control. Choose relationships!

When you look back

Kevin Heath wisely said that as your children grow they may forget what you said, but *they won't forget how you made them feel*. I ask parents of grown-up children: 'If you would do it all again, what would you change in the way you parented?'. This quote from Diane Loomans, an author and speaker on parenting, summarises all their answers:

'If I had my child to raise all over again, I'd build self-esteem first, and the house later. I'd finger-paint more, and point the finger less. I would do less correcting and more connecting. I'd take my eyes off my watch, and watch with my eyes. I'd take more hikes and fly more kites. I'd stop playing serious, and seriously play. I would run through more fields and gaze at more stars. I'd do more hugging and less tugging.'

If I meet you thirty years from now, what would you say you wish you had done differently?

Whatever it is, begin it today.

Point toward progress

I found that I must continue to remind myself that this is not about perfection, but rather about progress in the right direction. If I am less reactive and more consciously connected, then I am on the right path and headed in the right direction!—Marcia Ferstenfeld

Parents these days expect far too much from themselves, which (consciously or unconsciously) manifests itself in high expectations of our children.

By reminding ourselves that parenthood is not about perfection, but about *progress* in the right direction, we can reduce some of the pressure that our own expectations place on our children.

- 11 -
Self-disclosure time

To bring up a child in the way he should go, travel that way yourself once in a while.
Josh Billings

God grant me the serenity to accept the people I cannot change, the courage to change the one I can, and the wisdom to know it's me.
Unknown source

Feelings as clues

In my consultation sessions, I ask parents: 'If I freeze the clock in the most triggered moments you have with your child, how would you feel?' In response, they use single words to describe their feelings. Feelings never start with 'I feel that she –'. Instead, they are just one word, like 'angry'.

What do you feel in your challenging moments? Is it anger? If so, what's underneath that anger? Anger is often a secondary emotion, with something deeper underneath.

Name and write down at least three of your one-word feelings (e.g. disappointed, sad, frustrated, tired, furious, scared, out-of-control, helpless, desperate). Why is this important? Because many times children unconsciously communicate how they feel by creating those feelings in us.

Now ask yourself whether this could be how you child feels? And if so, why? This information can help you bring more empathy to the challenging moments.

Letting go

Sometimes parents have the best intentions for their children, yet come across as being very controlling.

- Do you speak *over* your child?
- Do you correct, advise or criticise them often?

This is tiring for you, and it is not effective for your children. It's time to let go. If you feel stressed, it can mean you are 'holding on' too much. Imagine yourself slowly relaxing your attitude, in a way that allows you to show more trust in your children. This means staying calm when things don't happen as you want, or expect them to. It means saying to yourself 'It is what it is and that's okay.' It means receiving what doesn't work with a thank you. It also means relaxing your expectations.

Your past in the present

If there is anything that we wish to change in the child, we should first examine it and see whether it is not something that could better be changed in ourselves—Carl Jung

What lingers from the parent's individual past, unresolved or incomplete, often becomes part of her or his irrational parenting—Virginia Satir

'He's not an achiever. He doesn't like to study and doesn't make any effort. What can I do?' asked one mother privately after my Growing Motivation lecture. I guessed that she was a high achiever and asked how she became that way. She said she admired and learned from her father, a very successful businessman. 'And your mother?' I asked. 'Mum was weak. An underachiever,' she said softly. After a moment of silence, she said, 'I always knew I didn't want to be like mum.' No wonder she's worried about her child's achievements!

We bring our own insecurities from our past to the present. When you feel very strongly about something, ask yourself: 'Where does this feeling come from?' A parent who is extremely anxious to force his way told me how it felt to be raised with a controlling father. Another told me he overreacts to his child throwing food, then explained that he was raised in poverty. The more strongly you feel about something, the more likely that your child will, unconsciously, react to that. Understand where this issue is coming from – it's a good start for the change to come.

Share the real you

'But I don't like playing with dolls, and that's what my daughter loves to do!' said Sophia in a parenting class. 'Who said that you need to?' I asked. Yes, it is nice (and effective) to enter your child's inner world by joining them in their favourite activities, but it's just as important for you to be genuinely interested, enjoying the moment and the time you spend together. Why not bring your child into your inner world too?

Where do you have passion? Where do you feel in your zone? Maybe it's something you liked to play when you were young, or something you have always wanted to try but haven't found the time. It might be something related to your profession. An architect couple once told me they loved taking their children to 'architecture for children' activities.

You all have strengths in your personality. So find those positive traits and use them to help you cope with challenges. Are you very comfortable with hugs? Then offer them in difficult situations. Do you have a great sense of humour? Use it to lighten up a situation (but never with sarcasm or at your children's expense). Are you a very sporty person? Offer to do activities with your children Whatever your strengths are, let them shine.

The future is now

I'd like to invite you to see the future, to look at the Big Picture. If in twenty years' time, your child turns to a therapist for support in a challenging time, what do you think they will say about you? How will they remember you from when they were young? What do you think they will say was the most important thing to you back then, as a parent *and* as a person?

Now come back to the present. It is your present. If change is needed, it's never too late! Consider how you can be more of the parent you want them to remember you as.

- What would that look like?
- What would you do that is different?
- Is your behaviour loving and accepting of who your children are, with their strengths and weaknesses, in their joyful moments and frustrating ones?

You can be the parent you want them to remember if you start now.

Rewrite the script

In between every action and reaction, there is a space. Usually the space is extremely small because we react so quickly, but take notice of that space and expand it. Be aware in that space that you have a choice to make. You can choose how to respond, and choose wisely, because the next step you take will teach your child how to handle anger and could either strengthen or damage your relationship—*Rebecca Eanes*

You're the main actor in a show. Which show, you ask? The show of Your Life. You have developed scripts for this show that you and your children adopt again and again. You each know how it's going to start, what follows what, and how it's going to end up. If you're not happy about your script, you – as the parent – hold the responsibility to change it.

The key is to understand that some of your reactions – whether they are avoiding or overreacting – put more petrol on the fire, while others help to subdue the flames.

You don't communicate core values when you are 'reactive'. Understanding that you don't need to react immediately to a child's behaviour is very empowering. You can control your reaction, and face the issue at another time, when you've had time to digest the situation, gain some clarity, and plan your actions calmly. Then rewrite your script with an act of connection.

Mirror your children's thoughts and feelings (Chapter 6); acknowledge their frustration; offer a hug. This won't only help them in the moment, but actually creates the script for the future.

Search the positive past

Sometimes we're so concerned about giving our children what we never had growing up, we neglect to give them what we did have growing up—James Dobson

We all bring some unmet needs and longing to our parenting experience, but let's not forget all the *good* experiences as well. What did you love about your parents and family when growing up? What would you like to pass down to the next generation? Even negative experiences (I'm not talking about traumatic events) helped develop some of your personality strengths. Tony Robbins, the American businessman, author and philanthropist says:

> 'I'm not saying not to blame your parents. But blame them for the positive things as well.'

This balance is healthy, not just for your children, but for you too. We want our children to look at us in thirty years time with compassion. Our parents did their best with the knowledge, emotional intelligence, and life experiences they had, and they did much better than their parents! We're doing much better than them! And our children will do even better than us. So remember the positive as well.

Caring for the caregiver

The most important thing that parents can teach their children is how to get along without them—Frank A. Clark

I believe that everything we do as parents in an exaggerated way (being overprotective, overly strict, overfeeding, etc.) is, in some way, a compensation for feelings of some lack we experienced in a different aspect of our own life. Diane came to see me regarding her eight-year-old daughter's 'restless' energy during the day. She acknowledged that she is an overprotective mother. I asked about the child's sleeping habits, and was told that she slept with Diane because her father travelled a lot – and Diane admitted to being afraid of sleeping by herself. Slowly she came to realise that it was her need for emotional and physical closeness – not her daughter's. Her daughter was more then ready to sleep by herself, and when she began doing so, it improved her energy during the day and enabled her to be more independent in other areas of life. Diane needed to expand her support system with other adults.

- Can you recognise any areas of parenting that you deal with in an *exaggerated* way? Maybe today is the day to start achieving a balance.
- What are your core needs? Are you fulfilling those needs with other adults, perhaps a partner, a friend or someone in your family?
- How can you take care of yourself so that it won't be at your child's expense?

When the problem becomes the pattern

If you really want a change in the family dynamic, but find it very difficult to change the way you react, it might be because you are too attached to the problem. If you think about it, and cognitively understand what needs to be done to improve the situation, then why is it so hard? What's in the way between you and making the changes you want? What keeps you attached to old ideas and behaviours?

I can tell you what. In many cases, there is some unconscious reason for the 'stuckness'. Your behaviour serves your old, learned patterns of parenting or connecting. Try to write down the problem. What do you understand and what would you like to improve about it? Now imagine thirty years from now: your child comes to you for parenting advice about the exact same problem you wrote down. What would you tell them? How do you guide or advise them?

This is your inner wisdom. You know what needs to be done. Use that wisdom and do it now.

Taking a look at timing

Children are our second chance to have a great parent–child relationship—Laura Schlessinger

We were on holiday with friends. My daughter, then seven and a half, challenged me like never before! I was very reactive at that time and not able to connect with her. Even now, years later, when I remember it, the pain, sadness and regret of that episode hits me hard. Several days later afterwards, I explored with my husband what really happened. Why did my usually easy, positive relationship with her start to challenge me at that precise moment? We were the same mother and daughter, so what happened?

I remembered the Imago theory that says we often experience a challenge in parenthood when our child is at an age when we ourselves were wounded, or stuck, by a lack of connection. Then I remembered that when I was seven and a half, my little brother was born, and in the same month, we also moved to a bigger house, and my beloved grandma became ill and died. With all these significant life-changing events, one assumes I was not the focus, to say the least.

I understood that something about the lack of my parent's availability at that age was replicated by my difficulty being present and available to my child's emotional need at the same age. So what did I do? With my husband's support, I went back to the basics of positive parenting. It's all in *Part One* of this book.

Mirror image

Children have never been very good at listening to their elders, but
they have never failed to imitate them—*James Baldwin*

Don't worry that children never listen to you; worry that they are
always watching you—*Robert Fulghum*

We expect a lot from our children today, but unfortunately we don't always
provide a good example. Your child learns from you long before they start
speaking. They observe everything! Even things you might not be aware that
you're doing – facial expressions, tone of voice, body posture.

Do you want your child to be more respectful, polite, present and patient?

Then have a look at what you're modelling. Your children don't learn from what
you tell them, but from what they *see*.

If you tell them not to lie and then tell your partner to answer the phone and say
you're not at home, your child learns to lie! Then you say 'It's not good to lie'!
Some parents complain about their children being glued to their screens, but
look at their smart phones constantly (even during sessions and workshops)!

- When you ask a stranger to bring you something, you probably say 'please'
  and 'thank you', but do you do the same at home when you ask your
  partner for a glass of water. Do you take such help for granted?
- When you shout 'Don't shout!' at our children, what do they really hear?
- How many times have you promised something, but not followed up on
  it? What do your children learn? They learn: '*You can say but not do.*'

Many parents come to me when they see some behaviour they don't like in
themselves in their children. It's like a mirror – and now they can see themselves.

The good news is, what we can see – we can change.

Be the model.

- 12 -
The echo of your words

Children are educated by what the grown-up is and not by his talk.
Carl Jung

This chapter gives priceless insights into the words that parents tend to use over and over again, that often lead to power struggles in the family, rather than fostering connections.

"Yes", "No" or "Maybe so"

Every parent is familiar with the situation where their child asks for something and the '*No*' answer is going to open an endless conflict. You have your own reasons for that answer, whether your child's needs conflict with your own, or for other boundary-related reasons. Next time this happens, remember that you don't have to answer with a '*Yes*' or '*No*'. The magic words can be:

'You are asking for a biscuit now. Hmmm, let me think about that'.

This gives you time to consider, and sends the message that you take the request seriously, which respects the child and helps if there is a 'No' answer later). At that moment it prevents any conflict. Try it. It works!

"I told you so"

You told your son not to climb on a box. One second later, he fell from the box. What do you say? What is your instinctive response? Most parents say, 'I told you so!' I'd like to offer a different response. It's not about right or wrong, or about the 'I know' attitude. Children were born with curiosity to try things out their own way. When they are hurt, hug them softly and say:

'It's not nice to fall like that' and 'What will help you? Maybe a kiss?'

Later on that day, talk with them about what you expected when you told them not to do the thing that hurt them. Remember, when children get older and choose to do something against your recommendation (like dating an undesirable partner!), you still want to be there for them in case they are emotionally hurt. Knowing from an early age that their parents usually say '*I told you so!*' produces teenagers who look for comfort elsewhere.

We want to be there for them! Start now.

The frequency of "No"

Children hear a great deal of the word 'No' during their day (*No picking your nose ... No speaking with your mouth full ... No jumping here ... No running ... No balls in the house*) and that's okay because they need to hear it from time to time. The problem is that when children (or adults!) hear too many 'No's it can create resentment and a power struggle. Sometimes you can just say 'No', but many times you can frame it differently.

'Mum, can I go and play now?'
'Yes, after we all clear the table.'

'Dad, can we play football outside?'
'Yes, after we tidy up the Monopoly.'

'Can I have a story?'
'Yes, you've had your bath so all you have to do now is brush your teeth.'

Can you see the difference?

Good and bad – there's no such thing

There's no such thing as a 'bad boy' or a 'bad girl' or 'not a good child'. There is a child who *feels* badly or who does not feel good about himself or herself. I often hear new mothers say things like 'She's a good baby. She doesn't cry a lot. She sleeps at night.' Does this mean that a baby who cries, for reasons of colic or hunger, is a '*bad* baby'?

This language of 'bad' and 'good' doesn't stop at the toddler years. One mother who came to see me explained that her twelve-year-old son was the 'bad child' in his class and the head teacher called her about him bullying others. There is no doubt he needed to learn limits and how to show empathy towards others and take responsibility for his actions, however, on an emotional level, it seemed clear that he didn't feel good about himself.

I explored this idea with his mother. She explained that he was overweight and that a family member called him 'fat'; and his father had left them a year before things kicked off at school. It wouldn't be enough to address only on his limits, boundaries and empathy – the mother and the school need to work together to help him feel better about himself.

Children who feel good about themselves make others feel good in their presence.

When it's not about love

Is this scene familiar to you?

Parent: 'Why did you do it? I asked you three times not to!'
Child: 'You don't love me!'
Parent: 'Of course I love you.'
Child: 'No you don't! You love her more.'
Parent: 'I love you a lot, even when I am angry.
Child: 'No you don't.'
Parent: 'Of course I love you. You're my son!'

Note how easily children can turn the parent's attention away from their behaviour to being defensive about how much they're loved. Yes, they are clever! And they read us like an open book. Next time, you can say:

'We're not talking about love now. We can talk about that later, if you want. Now we're talking about your behaviour. I asked three times for something and I expect you to listen.'

Can you see the difference?

A mistake or bravery?

I was on my way to work when I saw in the distance a young toddler who, in an attempt to walk by himself, tumbled and fell. By the time I passed them, his mother (or nanny), who was probably frustrated because he was still crying after she hugged him, held his hand and told him, 'I told you to hold my hand, honey. You need to think before you do things.' And they kept walking together while the toddler still cried. What did she actually tell him?

The hidden message was 'You're not capable. You need me. You don't think before you do things. Don't trust your instincts. Falling is your fault'.

How about saying this instead:

'It hurts when we fall. Do you want a hug? It was very brave to walk by yourself.'

And the message now:

'You are brave. It can hurt. (*Some connection might help e.g. a hug*) It's good to follow your instincts.'

This week, be mindful about what comes out of your mouth. Are you seeing and communicating mistakes or encouraging bravery?

Speak words of trust

Let's see if the words you use are in line with the message you want to pass on to your children. Your child forgets to take some homework to school, even though you said endless times 'Don't forget your homework. Put it in your bag now – if you don't you'll forget it'. What do you say? Many parents say 'I told you to put it in the bag. I knew this would happen.'

And if the same child, the following week, did all of his homework for once – without you telling him – what would you say? Many parents would be surprised, pleased and proud, but then say with surprise, 'Wow! I can't believe it! You did it by yourself! Well done!'

Now, consider the messages behind these sentences. The message behind the first one is: 'I knew this was going to happen. I didn't trust you to do better'. And the message behind the second is: 'I'm really surprised you did that. I didn't expect you to do better'. I'd like you to try to be aware of messages like this, and change them.

- When your children don't do well – be *surprised*! As if to say it's not in line with their 'better' self.
- And when they do well, acknowledge it, but with the *confidence* rather than surprise, and show that you know that was what you expected from them, because you know they can handle their responsibilities. No surprise there!

In both situations, we must hold the image of the *better* side of our children, so they can see themselves like that as well.

Speak to the "better self"

There is a famous exercise in which you show people a blank page with a small black dot in the middle of it and ask them what they see. Most people say 'a black dot'. Few mention the white page.

How is it so easy to ignore a whole page?

It reminds of the times I ask parents during an initial consultation session about their child's strengths. Many answer briefly, then give a long description of what needs to be changed. It's like it's easier to notice and remark on the negative than on the positive. To make a change you need to change your focus.

Your child, like you, has many parts. Speak to the better part.

It's not what you say, it's the way that you say it!

You can hear a piece of music that has no words and have a powerful emotional reaction to it – of sadness or fear, relaxation or joy. Do you know that there is also a rhythm to your words? The way you use your tone of voice, the pace of your speech, and the words you use all send important messages to your child.

One of the mothers in my parenting groups, Elena, said of her three-year-old son 'I said all the right things but he was still very aggressive'.

I suggested doing role play – her playing herself and another mother from the group playing her son, Jed. When we asked the Jed-mother how she felt afterwards, it became clear there was a disconnect between Elena's words and tone. She used a very apologetic approach and came across as a parent who was not secure. Her words communicated that the behaviour was not acceptable although they spelled out acceptable options for Jed to express how he felt, but her tone of voice gave a different message. It was how she said it. She gave the impression she was afraid or desperate, unsure of her approach, or uncomfortable telling him off.

We experimented with different tones of voice until her 'non-symbolic' communication was in line with her message. The following week, she reported that now just the way she looked at her son made a difference.

Does your non-symbolic communication fit the messages you're trying to convey? Are you being congruent – in sync?

The wolf of the heart

In this Native American story a grandfather was talking to his grandson about how he felt.

> Grandfather: 'I feel as if I have two wolves fighting in my heart. One wolf is a vengeful, angry, violent one. The other is a loving, compassionate one.'
>
> Grandson: 'Which wolf will win the fight in your heart?'
>
> Grandfather: 'The one I feed.'

I'll leave you with that thought.

- 13 -

Transitions: Change from the child's perspective

Transitions themselves are not the issue, but how well you respond to their challenges!
Jim George

Here the focus is on the ways that you can support your children in day-to-day 'transitions' which include things like separation anxiety, moving house or school, and having to stop playing to go out somewhere.

Mood music

Music is the shorthand of emotion—Leo Tolstoy

Where words fail, music speaks—Hans Christian Andersen

When you want to change the atmosphere or energy at home, use music! It could be a vibrant, high-energy one, or one you know that brings a smile to your children's faces in the morning. Likewise, use calming, (yoga-style) music before bedtime or when you want them to 'slow down' after a high-energy activity. Did you know, you can also play music to help your children move from one emotional mood to another? If your child comes home stressed from school – play something relaxing. Low self-esteem? Choose age-appropriate songs with empowering words. Music works in two ways – when you feel something, you can play music to deepen and connect with that emotion, or when you want to change the way you feel, you can play music that will 'take you there'. Whatever way you make use of music, play it on a regular basis at home.

Touch points ease transition

Hugging and touching children during the day's main point of transition can help reduce their anxiety. Appropriate and healthy touch *heals*. Try to make it a part of your routine to hug, cuddle, kiss, or just touch their shoulder (with avoidant teens), when waking up in the morning, before one of you leaves the house, when you reunite, and before bedtime. All these points in the day have the potential to create anxiety, so introducing a 'comfort touch', even for seconds, can create a big difference.

Changing the channel

When you want to move from one activity to another, especially from a high-energy activity to a more relaxing one (such as dinner or bath), use this game to help your children concentrate.

> Tell them to be very, very, quiet because you're going to open the window or door and they need to listen very carefully because when you close it, they will need to tell you all the things they heard.

> Do it twice in a row, giving them enough time to pick up on different sounds – two or three minutes each time.

Now your children are ready to shift activity.

Raising resilience

There is a metaphor about waves and water. If you are a wave there is a fear you will disappear. If you understand that you are the water, then you have no fear. The wave passes, but the water stays.

Some children have a fear of change – going from a small class into the lunch hall with the whole school; leaving home to go to school each morning; moving house or starting a new afterschool club. How can we help our children understand that they are the water? How we can help them develop resilience – the capacity to recover quickly from difficulties?

Many of the tips in this book develop resilience. but I'd like to give you a specific one here to use when your children are anxious about a change:

> Simply remind them of a similar situation in the past which they coped successfully with.

Maya noticed her daughter was concerned about starting a new art class. She said: 'It can be scary to start a new class where you don't know the other children. I remember how last weekend you made new friends in the playground. You were less than five minutes in the playground and you came back with a lovely friend! She was shy and you had the courage to go to her and offer to play'.

I like to remind my daughter of her courage to go on the roller-coaster again and again. When parents remind their children of situations in which they have shined, it forms an inner image that helps them see the situation as a wave. It will pass. And their qualities or courage, patience, or whatever, will (like the water) stay and be integrated as part of who they are.

Create a mantra

To help children with separation anxiety, I recommend parents create a sentence with them and repeat it in every similar situation. For example, when separating for a night's sleep, they can develop their own mantra – something along the lines of:

'Good night, sweet dreams, I love you very much, kiss-kiss, see you in the morning.'

And you say it as well. With time, it becomes a code for safe separation because when it is repeated they get a sense of control.

The same can be done with a child who finds it difficult to separate when going to school.

'Have a lovely day, I'll think about you and see you at pick up'.

You may have noticed that I end the sentences with the *reunion* – morning or pick up – in order to indicate a *limit* to the separation period for them and provide an anchor for safety. Having an end to the separation makes it easy to contain.

Breathe easy

Obviously we all breathe, but not necessarily in a conscious way. In my clinic, I teach children with anxiety or anger issues how to breathe using cotton-wool or a feather. First, I demonstrate by modelling and then invite them to join in.

I explain that we're going to breathe fully into our belly (touching my belly with two hands), chest (moving my hands to my chest) and throat (placing my hands on my throat and taking a breath in).

Next, we bring our hands with the cotton-wool (or feather) very close to our mouths and exhale very slowly so that the cotton-wool (or feather) doesn't move at all!

We repeat it five to seven times, and the child gets great sense of calm and relaxation.

Teach this at a quiet time and invite your children to keep the cotton-wool (or feather) and practice whenever they feel the need. They can use it before going to sleep, when they feel angry or when they just want to relax.

Morning with Buddha

One of my clients said that every morning, after breakfast, she and her two little children sit on the carpet and make an 'Ohmmmm...' sound for several minutes.

This is such a creative way to give the body positive vibrations and can lead to a calm start to the day. She said that although it takes them a couple of minutes to perform, they like the feeling that follows, and they are more focused and proactive.

For some children, and adults, doing things like breathing or 'Ohmmmm...' makes them laugh. But laughter is energy! Welcome it when it happens as your children learn the new skill. It might relate to nervousness, embarrassment, or simply because it's funny for them.

Tell them to laugh as much as they want! Let them expand their energy and joy.

Is it normal?

Many of the parents who come to see me describe their children's behaviour and ask 'Is that normal?'. Most of the time, my answer is 'Yes'. Interestingly, the issue is usually related to one of two emotions: anxiety or over-excitement. In the case of anxiety, or fear, it's not enough to 'fix' the behaviour because the behaviour is not the problem. It's merely a symptom.

Children react in ways that look strange to us for any number of reasons. However, on a deeper level, the theme for all is the feeling of disconnection with their caregiver or parent. Understanding things from their point of view, and helping them to express how they feel in the appropriate and healthy way – while still being in connection with them – is the solution. Don't label anything as abnormal (*You're not behaving like a normal boy!*), rather, talk with them about the pain they're experiencing – without giving it a name (normal or otherwise). Just say:

'I can see that you are very upset'.

Don't assume you know your child, either. In their reality, their behaviour makes sense. Even if some of the time you decide to ignore their negative behaviour, be aware that the underlying issue still needs to be addressed.

You will find many techniques in this book, and on-line, but if you feel that there's no improvement, please don't wait. Look for a local parent advisor or therapist who can guide you. It is normal for a jealous, frustrated or sad child to say hurtful things or behave inappropriately for their age. Does it make a difference that it's normal? No. They need your help and support either way.

Talk about expectations

'We can't go with him to a restaurant. He doesn't sit still, makes lots of noises, runs around, disturbs everyone around us. It's so embarrassing that we regret leaving the house', said Emma. She was desperate, and like many parents I see in my clinic, she identified a specific place that her child finds it challenging to accommodate.

What is really helpful in these situations is to prepare children in advance for the wanted behaviour. For example, taking advantage of the drive or walk to the restaurant, Emma could tell her son that they're going to eat out and ask how he thinks it will be sensible to behave when they're there. She could also encourage him to say what he can do – as opposed to what he can't do. He could bring a book or something to colour in. They could use the time between the order and serving to share about their day, or make up stories together. Even suggesting a run-around before or after the restaurant (on the way there or back) would allow him to release some energy. This will be especially useful for children transitioning from a quiet activity.

It's like having a relationship with an adult – preparation and talking about expectations can make a huge difference.

Present the dilemma

Instead of getting locked into a power struggle with your children, you can try using the 'present the dilemma' approach. Rather than saying 'Yes' or 'No' to complicated requests, you can start an open and respectful dialogue that describes both sides of your dilemma. The following are examples. For a child who finds it difficult to leave play dates:

Child: 'Mum, can I go for a play with Simon today?'

Parent: 'I'm happy for you to go. We also need to be at home by five-thirty for a delivery. How do you think we can work it out?'

For a teenager who is becoming more independent:

Child: 'Dad, can I go with my friends to a party?'

'Parent: I have a dilemma. On one hand, I'd like you to have fun with your friends. On the other, I need to know you're safe. What do you suggest we do?'

By inviting your children to be part of the solution, as explained previously, you can often avoid unnecessary conflict and encourage their ability to cooperate and make positive choices.

- 14 -
Routine rules

Routine is liberating, it makes you feel in control.
Carol Shields

When you have a routine, you have good habits. When you have good habits, you have a peaceful state of mind! Here I will explore many ways for you to establish exactly that. In every lecture, there are parents who express their tiredness, frustration and helplessness when dealing with the early morning routine before school or in the evenings before bedtime. Let's introduce some order in the home using some simple and effective tips to make it a little easier.

Set up for success

Find a good time for you and your children (when you're all fed, rested and relaxed), to share that you don't feel good when everyone is stressed in the morning before going to school. Tell them *briefly* how you feel when you leave the house that way and that you assume it doesn't feel good for them either. They'll hear only a few sentences and then their minds will wander off – so choose your words carefully. You could ask them how they feel about it. Then explain that they're big enough to be responsible for being ready in the morning and that you want to do some fun activity together to help everyone feel good when they leave the house.

- On a piece of paper invite them to write (do the writing for them if they can't yet) or draw what needs to be done in the morning. Give them space and time to bring their own wisdom. They might list things in a different order to the one you have in mind, and may include activities such as playing, watching TV and eating. Don't interfere. Then work together to agree and order their priorities. Still together, create a large poster-sized piece of card and list all the tasks in the agreed order. Again, encourage them to be very active in making it. Tell them that from now on, in the morning, they need to check the list to make sure that they've completed all of the agreed tasks before doing other activities on the list, like playing.

The next morning, when your child switches on the TV out of sequence, you say:

'I see that you've already brushed your teeth. Go and check on your list what else we need to do before watching TV'.

Some children like to add a check sign to every activity they completed. Regardless, it becomes their responsibility, not yours. The same process can be applied for bedtime.

Silence the screens

Many parents' challenges during the morning and evening routines are the result of 'screen time'. Eliminating screen time on TV, iPads, smart phones, computers, etc. during these times can solve a host of problems. In the mornings, children enter a different world when they watch screens, and with their attention fixed like that it can be very challenging to get them to complete all their morning tasks in the rush to school.

There are even more reasons why it isn't healthy for children to have screen time in the evening, before bedtime. We now know that it causes children to have less deep sleep, poorer concentration the following day, more bad dreams, and an overall higher level of anxiety and aggressiveness. For one thing, it's over-stimulating for the brain, and children find it challenging to neutralise and calm themselves down for a good night's sleep. From the time you start the bedtime routine (dinner, shower, etc.), leave the screens out of reach.

Waking up with music

In my home there is a sign for getting dressed in the morning. At eight o'clock I play a song – a different one each day. The music is the sign that it's time to get dressed, brush our teeth and come for breakfast. This is one of our habits I appreciate the most. No arguments, no one needs to be the policeman, there's no dragging around, asking over and over again. Music, clothes, teeth, then arriving at breakfast together. If we finish our breakfast early, we have time to play, read a story, dance or plan our day.

You might read this and say: that won't happen in my house! A response that reminds me of the quote of unknown source: 'It's impossible,' said Pride. 'It's risky,' said Experience. 'It's pointless,' said Reason. 'Give it a try,' whispered The Heart.

So give it a try! You need to introduce the idea at a relaxed time during the day, not in the morning. Explain that you heard about how nice is it to wake up in the morning with music playing, and add:

> 'Because you are big and capable, you don't need me as your police-man. The music will be our code – when you hear the music, you just need to dress, brush your teeth and come for breakfast. Is there a song you prefer to hear first? Do you want to practice this now or in the morning?'

You will still need to encourage them during the first few days, however with positive and effective encouragement you will be on the right track for easy and stress-free mornings.

The role of routine?

For babies and through childhood, a routine creates expectations and a sense of control, which helps children to contain and cope with the uncertainties of life.

Most of a child's life is out of their control, which creates anxiety. But having a healthy routine, helps them retain a sense of control. They know what to expect and when to expect it, and this provides a great deal of comfort and safety. You experience this when you take a newborn on holiday with you. Although they're very young, they react to the changes in smell, temperature, even texture of the sheets, because they are out of their routine. And this creates stress, which means that they need comforting and reassurance before they can sleep. If you do need to take a baby or child out of their routine, be prepared (this is addressed in the next tip).

There can be exceptions. You might relax the bedtime routine or specific diet on holidays, or allow for treats and indulgences that are not usually in the family routine, when spending time with grandparents, for example, and on special occasions.

Have space for fun

'He doesn't listen! He is so challenging, I find that I don't like to be with him any more,' said an honest and frustrated Gabriela about her middle son. I hear this often (and more so regarding middle children). Thus starts a spiral of negative actions and reactions, full of tension and negativity. So I asked: 'When was the last time you had fun together?'

It's important to have a routine of fun in the family. Some people like cooking together, others dancing. Some like to do silly things like making faces or acting, and others find the fun in art or outdoor activities.

Whatever it is, make sure you include it in your routine. The ideal option will be to combine the obligatory routine with fun. Here are some ideas that you might be able to use:

- Brushing teeth in a 'game' style.
- Cooking a healthy meal together.
- Getting dressed while dancing.
- Tidying up toys for a game.
- Finding pairs of socks in the laundry basket.

Just think creatively and make sure you have a routine for fun during your day.

Routine breaks

Before instigating a change of routine, if you're all going away, for example, talk to your children and explain what's going on – even to babies. Babies understand your energy even before they understand your words, and talking to them is in itself a great habit because it develops their language and understanding of the world.

When you speak with children about what has happened, and what's going to happen, life sounds logical and reasonable, and makes more sense. Your voice and touch are a great source of safety at holiday times. There's a lot in the connection created beyond words.

Consider taking their sheets with you, a special teddy or 'attached' object, a favourite food or something you believe will help them settle. Whenever possible, and especially at the start of the holiday, try to keep babies routines similar to home. It will help them hold within all the other changes around them. Also use every opportunity to talk about the differences they notice.

The good of the gong

When listening to Thich Nhat Hanh, the famous Zen Buddhist monk from Vietnam, talking about mindfulness, there was a dong sound from a gong. He explained that whenever it sounds, everyone stops whatever they are doing to take three mindful breaths. It means stopping what you are doing and being in that moment. It means noticing your breath, your body movement, your heartbeat, and telling yourself and noticing that you are inhaling and exhaling, and connecting with your body.

When one does this enough times it becomes a habit: *Dong = notice three breaths.*

What a great habit to have at home!

Why not buy a gong or use a different instrument (wooden spoon on a pan!) to create this effect at home? Explain to your children that when someone sounds the gong, everyone stops whatever they are doing to breathe mindfully three times.

Don't use this only to quieten your child, but randomly throughout the day. Sound it also when you feel triggered by your child – not for your child, but for you!

After three deep breaths you will react differently. It brings peace within.

Change your role

Having a routine doesn't mean that you need to be the policeman. You are the family *coach*, guiding them with peace and empowerment. Imagine that between your children and yourself there is a space of energy waves. When you try to lead your children to be ready for school or to go to sleep, how do you imagine these energies in the space between you? Do the waves slap together? Is there a vacuum between them? Are they facing the same direction or each one against the other?

Your task is to change the direction of your own energy wave so that it goes alongside your children's. This way you are together facing the task ahead.

For the next few days, make a diary of what you say to encourage your child with routine tasks. Then read it out loud. Are you the 'policeman' at home?

Bedtime – trick or a treat?

Children are masters at stretching time before going to sleep. They want a drink. They are hungry. They need the toilet again. Every parent is familiar with this. I've also heard parents describe the situation where their shy child suddenly wants to talk and talk about what happened at school, or their feelings or fears. Possibly another way to delay not going to sleep?

However, it's not that different for adults – the day's worries, anxieties and concerns often spring to mind the moment our heads touch a pillow! It's as if the entire nervous system relaxes and all the worries from past, present and future are allowed to flow through.

Children are the same. They need intimate time with their parents before going to sleep to communicate whatever might be preoccupying them. It helps them regulate their emotions and prepare themselves for a good night's sleep.

Bedtime is a time to feel connected, where separation is marked by a hug and tucking in – regardless of their age. You can set your own time-frame for each child before they go to sleep, maybe a story and five or ten minutes of talking before tucking in. If you feel this stretches it out too much, why not start the bedtime routine half an hour earlier, so that you don't need to rush?

Making the most of mealtimes

Getting together for daily (even weekly!) family mealtimes are far less common these days – which is very unfortunate. When there is an opportunity to eat together, parents often make the mistake of commenting more about their children's eating habits than anything else.

Family mealtime is an opportunity to share things – at any age. In my family, we share about our day, we plan for the day or weekend ahead, we talk about interesting things we've read or heard, share our thoughts, feelings and opinions about specific topics, or tell jokes.

Mealtimes are not the time to educate or comment about why children don't eat this or that. If you must comment on their eating habits, minimise it so that it isn't the focus of your time together. Comments such as 'I like it when you try new food' or 'It's important for your body to eat healthy food. I hope you'll find something you want to try today' are more encouraging than '*Why do you always only ...*' or '*You need to finish what's on your plate whether you like it or not*'.

Remember that when the pressure to eat is lower, there is a higher chance that they will eat!

If you choose to talk about the food itself, encourage tasting (with repeated experiences children's palette become accustomed to different tastes) as well as conversation about the food, such as:

'Does it feel crunchy or smooth?'

'What do you think is in the sauce that made this taste?'

'Do you like raw carrots or cooked ones?'

'Which other food becomes soft when cooked? Which ones become harder?'

- 15 -
Sibling relationships

Siblings: children of the same parents, each of whom is perfectly
normal until they get together.
Sam Levenson

Your parents leave you too soon and your kids and spouse come along late, but
your siblings know you when you are in your most inchoate form.
Jeffrey Kluger

**Here you can find few tips about how to promote caring and positive
sibling relationships, including sensitivity and empathy toward
each other and a sense of team spirit.**

Play with positioning

Try to use play-date time to expand your child's experience with regards to
their position in the family. For example, make sure that older children have an
opportunity to play with children who are even older than them, and younger
children get play with children who are younger than them. This will expand
their experience at home by providing opportunities to both learn from and
lead others, respectively. What about the middle one (which in a more positive
way we call the 'centred' child)? Aha! They need a play date solely with you!

One at a time

Research shows that fifteen or twenty minutes of one-to-one time that parents
spend with each child every day significantly reduces sibling rivalry and
aggression. If you are like many of the parents in my groups, you will think
'How can I find time to do that?!'

The trick is to use everyday tasks at home to involve one child at a time. You
need to buy something from the supermarket? Take one of them. You want to
walk around the block for some fresh air? Take a child for company. You're
preparing dinner? Invite one of them to help you cook.

If the day passed by very quickly and you didn't get a chance for one-to-one
time, decide that today they will have separate bath times instead of bathing
them altogether. This way they don't need to fight constantly for your attention.

Celebrate siblings

Teach your children to create special moments for each other. Encourage them to make cards, wrap old games as presents, create arts and crafts for each other, or buy small gifts from their pocket money for birthdays and special occasions (a new school, finishing exams), or for no special reason.

You can also print out photos for them of them having fun or special moments together. They can create arts and crafts with them or an album to remember. Hanging a collage of sibling photos in a visible place at home will also keep reminding them of special moments together.

Beyond compare

*When we see a field of flowers we don't judge how some grow faster than others or are turned in a different direction. We notice their beauty. With children we assume they all grow at the same pace and be turned in the same direction. Instead we could choose to see the beauty of children just as they are—**Unknown source***

Praise and encourage your children only in comparison to their own achievements, not to those of other family members. For example, say: 'Wow! Today you walked from home to the supermarket! Well done!' rather than 'Wow! Today you walked from home to the supermarket like your sister!'

As Amy, a mother of three, said in one parenting class: 'You never forget moments when you were compared to others!'

This is so true.

Children become adults who still remember (and some still act out) the pain of being compared. If you think about it, they are being compared to others all day long at school, in afterschool clubs, with their extended family and when playing with friends.

Your home is the only place that values them for who they are – without comparing to others. One of your children might not do as well academically as you or your other children, but may have a special talent for art; they may not be athletic, but brilliant at chess.

Let your children feel special by identifying and acknowledging their unique achievements and progress with respect to themselves.

Feelings of fairness

When your child protests 'It's not fair' many parents reply *'Life's not fair'*. This message is lost on them and it denies their feelings. There's also a big chance it will be interpreted as 'Mum and dad are not fair!'

Sometimes when children complain about fairness, what they are really asking for is a compliment, a moment of devoted attention, or some kind of validation of their frustration.

Listen to the feelings behind the words. And acknowledge them.

For example, when a younger child says 'It is not fair Mia can go for a sleepover and I can't'. You can say:

> 'I hear that you're angry because you can't go for a sleepover yet. Mmm. I can understand that. In our house sleepovers are from the age of six years old. I'm sure you'd like to be six now.'

When children hear that there is a reason behind a decision, and it's given alongside validation about their feelings, they find it much easier to regulate their emotions.

Team teaching

Your child asks for help. Don't rush in to the rescue! If one of their siblings has the skills, refer the request to them.

Older children can help with zipping up coats or tying shoe laces, and this strengthens their important role in the family.

The younger ones also have many skills that can and *should* be used.

My little one, for example, found all sorts of things that we'd lost or misplaced at home once she'd learned how to crawl. She also helps us when we are in a hurry by bringing each family member their shoes.

Find what your younger ones do best and remember to refer siblings to them as well!

By doing this, you're not only teaching them the value of working together and using sibling resources for help and comfort, but you are also building teamwork and bonding experiences that will continue well into the future.

Be a coach (not a referee)

The 'hat' I wear as a couples' therapist and a mother is very similar. In both roles, the focus is on the relationship and not on the individuals. My client is not *either* partner, but the space between them. In the therapeutic process, I'm not the judge. I'm not taking sides, but serve to validate each point of view, trying to move the couple from a reactive mode to consciousness, connection, empathy and growth.

It's the same in your role as a parent to more than one child. Keep your focus on the relationship between your children, coaching them to resolve issues in appropriate ways.

How do you do that? If they argue, give them some time out to cool down (especially in heated situations), then sit with them and hear both sides. Validate both experiences by saying something like:

> 'I hear that you, Amy, feel very angry because Anna borrowed your top again. And I hear that you, Anna, are very surprised because you feel you give Amy many of your clothes.'

Then coach them to find a solution, rather than telling them who is right and who is wrong or how to fix the situation. In other words, teach them to solve their own conflicts in a healthy way. What better gift can you give your children?

Avoid the blame game

When your children have a conflict or fight with a sibling or a friend, avoid name-calling or passing judgement.

Instead, say what you see in the context of the 'house rules'. For example, instead of 'Jonathan, why did you hit your brother?' say:

> 'I see two children fighting. In our family we don't hit. If you're angry, say it with words.'

Instead of 'Rona, why did you take all the bread for yourself?' say:

> 'I see no bread left on the table. In our family we share food.'

Likewise, when one blames the other for something, say:

> 'In our family we don't blame each other.'

Just be aware of your own words next time your partner breaks a cup ... and remind yourself that in your family you don't blame others.

Cultivate caring

Express with words the value of siblings working together.

'Look how your sister helps you put on your shoes. She cares about you.'

'Your sister copies you. She wants to be exactly like you when she is big! That's how much she loves you!'

When they work together, praise them collectively, rather than individually. For example:

'You worked so well together to set the table and clear it up, now we have time to go to the park.'

Remember that when your words reflect what you *see* (rather than personality traits or outcomes), you add another dimension to their caring behaviour towards each other.

How the sun shines

Parents say that when their child asks 'Who do you love more, me or my sister?' they say 'I love you both the same' or 'I love you exactly as much as I love her'.

But what they *really* want to know is not who you love more, but that they are loved in a unique way. Express your unique love by saying:

'I love you both in very special ways.'

'You are the one and only you in my life and no-one will ever take your place.'

You can also mention the specific quality of that child, as in:

'You are my oldest, you made me a mum. No one else can be my oldest!'

My oldest one loves this and whenever she feels less appreciated she reminds me of it. I once heard a metaphor that a parent's love is like the sun. Sharing the sun does not mean that each one gets less, and a parent's love shines on their children just like the sun.

Remember, your children do not really want you to say who you love more. They are asking how you feel about them!

Beware of angels

In almost every family, there is the 'good' child. The angel child who, especially compared to other family members, requires the least attention, boundaries and direction, who is caring about others, who helps, who does well at school, who is sensitive and follows rules. The 'easy' one.

Be aware of this child. Sometimes they are the most vulnerable, in that they can pay the emotional price of being the 'invisible' child, the one with no *expressed* needs. See angels for who they are. Consider whether they are paying any price in the family and do something about it. See their core needs, give them your time and attention, and let them break the rules from time to time so that they can explore their identity and grow.

Mind the gap

Some children bring out the best in their parents and some press all their buttons. If you feel that your personality clashes with your child's, the key is not to let them interpret this as being a less-favoured child.

Once you acknowledge you have some personality issues with a child, make enough time to bond by being alone with him or her. Find the bridges between the two of you. What do both of you like doing? Which hobbies do you share? What does this child like doing that you admire or appreciate?

Do it together! It might be a cookery class, a photography course, some sporting activity, or learning a new musical instrument. Build new opportunities for communication. Give them the chance to impress you, to be acknowledged and, mainly, to feel connected.

Older angst

Two tips, seemingly in contrast to each other, are for older children in a family.

 Talk with your older child about the meaning of being the older sibling. Being the older one may mean more responsibilities and privileges. Also, because he is big, his little sister looks at him as a very important person in the family.

Let your older child *be a child*, not an adult. Saying '*You should know better!*' or '*You need to show an example!*' only builds resentment.

I remind parents that when their first one was four years old he seemed so big, but when the third one reached four, he is still the baby! It's our perception of the age, not the age itself, that we react to.

- 16 -
Parental authority

There are no facts, only interpretations.
Friedrich Nietzsche

What is your parenting style? Are you too strict? Too soft? Do you feel you have authority? Or do you feel your children are holding the family's steering wheel? In this chapter you will find some ideas about constructive authority and how to achieve that.

Safe means sound

Your task is to become a confident and safe parent so your children's confidence and self regulation can flourish. By being confident and safe – that is assertive without negativity (blaming, shaming, judgement) – then your child's big emotions can be contained and modified.

This is especially so when they challenge you and you are at risk of being over-emotional and reactive. You have a bigger goal. You're going to use it as an opportunity to share your core values. I will share with you one example.

One afternoon, arriving home after school pick-up after shopping in the local small supermarket, my daughter (then aged five) said she was going to be busy in her room. I was pleased to have several minutes alone to organise things around the house before discovering that there was a reason for her request for privacy. Apparently, she had taken a small package of sweets from the shop and put them in her pocket.

As you can imagine, I was very surprised and embarrassed. I took two deep breaths and said quietly, 'We don't take things from a shop without paying for them. It's called stealing. Now we need to do something kind for the shop-keeper to say sorry and we will give back the sweets and pay for them.'

With no argument, she said, 'I'll make him a card, but I don't want to go and give it to him.' To which I replied:

'I'm not happy about that. But I agree to take the card for you this time.
If it happens again, you will need to do it.'

She made a lovely card with a drawing and the word 'Sorry'. I went to the shop (hoping not to be seen by anyone I knew), apologised and paid. The man was so touched that since then he has welcomed my daughter with pleasure.

Trust yourself

Our parents made mistakes – but they did it with confidence! In the past, when the children were not the 'focus' of the family, parents often acted without knowing, but with authority. Today, I hear parents act in a way that they know is productive, but with hesitation and doubt. There are far too many advisors around for parents now – TV and radio shows, newspapers, books, family members and therapists. All this advice can be overwhelming, and can take over their intuition and undermine their confidence. 'Experts' frighten parents with the prospect of causing unhappy childhoods, and we are concerned about what they say, yet at the same time we look to them for the answers, as people who 'should know best'.

In the past, if children were fed and dressed, that meant their parents were good enough. Today, the standard of 'good parenting' is very high. The attempt to be better parents often results in the lack of boundaries. When you hesitate and are in doubt, you create anxiety in your children. In their experience, if you, the adults, don't know what to do, then who does? When children are in charge, it feels overwhelming, and ends in anarchy; a child who feels 'in charge' of a parent is more likely to experience high levels of anxiety and aggression. This, in turn, fulfils your unconscious fears.

Read, listen to advice, explore options, but then let your intuition guide you. Whatever makes sense to you, and you decide to do, do it with confidence.

Make a mantra

Positive thinking in challenging times might mean changing your view or fantasy about what it means to be a 'good parent'. Take the time to create a mantra for yourself, then write it down in several places and read it aloud to yourself whenever you need to. Examples of mantras I have heard over the years include:

- A good parent is not a parent who does for their children, but a parent who enables their children to do for themselves.
- A good parent is a not a parent who is never angry, but a parent who expresses anger without hurting their child's soul and mind.
- As a parent I'm aware of my feelings and take the time to think how to react.
- It's a stressful time. It will pass and all will be okay. See the opportunity and try to relax and let go.
- I'm a 'good enough' parent! Breathe! What would an ideal parent do now?

What's your mantra?

With the baby we gave birth to guilt

'We can't do that!' said the parents in front of me when I suggested they reduce some of their children's time on computers. 'We come back from work late, everyone needs to chill out and we don't want to start a "war". They don't see us enough anyway.' Welcome to guilt!

Many parents who come to me don't realise that what's behind most of their actions are their feelings of guilt! They think they were not present enough when their children were babies; they didn't hold them enough; they weren't good at placing boundaries or splitting their time between their children; they didn't like their personality; they missed a school play; they were late collecting them from school; and so on.

And what happens then? Usually, the parents want to compensate in some way. How? By giving over their abilities emotionally, physically or financially (e.g. gifts and afterschool clubs). And when parents give above and beyond their abilities they are likely to explode!

And what happens then?

Yes, you're right! They feel more guilt! They feel disappointed in their children and themselves, and the cycle starts again.

If you need to change something in your lifestyle to bring more balance, do that. We all need to create a new image for ourselves as a 'good enough' parent (phrased by Winnicott), which helps bring about balance between our needs, our children's needs, and our relationship's needs. But when you come home, leave guilt at the door.

Method to the madness

From early on, children know what they need to do. They are designed to develop. Let's think about babies of six or seven months old. They can't use their hands and fingers to explore objects; they can only hold them, not stroke, push, pull, or explore. However, they can control their mouths, tongues and lips – at that age their mouth area has more nerves per square millimetre than in any other part in their body. So if they want to know about an object (is it soft, solid, noisy, tasty, wet, round or square) they will put it in their mouth.

When parents complain that their baby puts everything in their mouths, I tell them that it is not only a natural exploration, it also shows development and growth and an interest in the world around them. The more they experience with their senses, the more they learn. Instead of being worried, the parents then understand that the baby is in the process of learning. So don't disturb them!

Knowing when to relax boundaries

Providing boundaries for children is an act of love. Boundaries are the way to transform your values into day-to-day life. You do need to choose your priorities, however. We can't expect to impose too many rules and limits and expect a relaxed and happy family life. You and your partner need to choose what is most important for you. Ask yourself why the measure you are thinking of is important, and concentrate on that. We can't fight with our children all day long about every aspect of life – hygiene, education, persistence at sticking with afterschool clubs, respecting others, hairstyles, clothing and tidying up.

An essential and perfectly ordinary part of growing is about exploring the boundaries. For example, one of my children is 'the good girl', and she has a strong sense of fairness. She is so ethical and 'by the book' that she sometimes puts her needs last. I remember the first time her teacher asked to talk with me. She said my daughter did something 'naughty' (I hate this word but I bring that up in a different tip). The teacher saw the big smile on my face! If she only knew how hard I'd worked for my daughter to do something 'outside the rules' she would understand why I saw this as progress. You know your child. You know whether you need to relax or to strengthen your boundaries.

Let the challenge be your lesson

When a client says to me '*I have a problem with my child*' I gently rephrase it to 'You have a challenge with … and this challenge also invites opportunity. What is the opportunity?' Can you see the difference in viewing the situation this way? Turning a 'problem' into a 'challenge and opportunity'? The first invites stuckness, the latter invites growth. When you experience tension in your family, the universe sends you a message: something in the challenge is here to tell you something about your child, or you or your relationship.

The reality is challenging, so you will stretch outside your comfort zone. The difficult situation is not necessarily a bad thing. If you're not frightened by it, and you are prepared to invest effort and faith, you are investing for the long term in yourself and your relationship. When we're able to contain our challenges and strong feelings and see things with clarity, we can understand the patterns that created the challenging situation. Then it will be clearer to see where and how we want to progress and grow. How do we get there?

You can start by writing down all the things you know about the challenge. Add your feelings around about it as well. Ask yourself 'Is there more to it?' and keep writing. Explore your main motive and thinking. When did you develop this way of thinking? Thinking about this challenge, what is your opportunity for growth? Reflect and let yourself wonder. It will become clearer.

Raise your words not your voice

Raise your words, not your voice. It is rain that grows flowers, not thunder—**Rumi**

When listening to a speech by the Buddhist monk Thich Nhat Hanh, I noticed that throughout he spoke in a very soft voice, almost whispering. There is something healing and calming about people who speak in low tones. I brought this idea back to my parenting course and challenged the parents to lower their voices with their children, especially when they want to be heard but don't feel their children are listening. Something very interesting happened. They reported back that the lower their voices, the more their children listened to them. Whenever they raised their voices, the children talked over them, or continued with their own activities or reacted uncooperatively. If you ask your child to clear the table, and it looks like you are being ignored, you may in the past have asked three times then shouted your request again or become angry. Now you have another option, to whisper several words: 'The table please'. Whispering doesn't mean giving in – I can whisper with an assertive attitude and confidence. When you whisper that way, children will, in most cases, automatically give you their attention.

What I love about this idea is that when I lost my voice after a cold, my children not only whispered back, but they became quiet 'within' so they were able to hear and cooperate.

What do they want to tell us?

I hear it all the time: '*My child wants sweets all day … My children want gifts from their dad when he is away … My daughter wants me to buy her more and more clothes … My son wants me to play with him all the time … My boy wants a TV in his room*'.

It reminds me what Haim Ginott, a clinical psychologist and author, used to say: 'Is it what he needs or what he *wants*? A child has many real needs which can and should be satisfied. His *wants* are a bottomless pit'.

It's impossible to expect parents to think about the need behind every child's request. Yet it may be beneficial for them to do so, especially if there are repetitive complaints from a child, and it can help you understand your child. The child who wants a TV in his room may need more privacy, or a sense of control or independence. All of this be fulfilled without a TV in the room, through open discussion, acknowledgment, validation and space to explore other options.

A child who wants sweets all day might need a moment of devoted attention, or may need boundaries, or help with self-regulation. So the next time you hear '*I want …*' try to identify the hidden need, and react to that.

The sign for restart

If you are like many parents who attend my workshops, you notice the lack of boundaries or authority when you're in the middle of a power struggle.

You ask your child to do something, and they refuse, or do the opposite. You try to say it again with more certainty, but it makes no difference. You might give up and move on, or keep asking or demanding that they obey. You might raise your voice, your intensity, or change your body language – your child does the same.

In such situations, to keep demanding doesn't add to your sense of authority.

Knowing that some things that you say and do add more flame to the fire, while others help to change the energy, is one piece of the solution.

Another part is to understand that your actions don't necessarily need to be at that same moment.

Saying something like:

> 'I'm not happy about what's going on here (or name the specific be-haviour without talking about the child in order to create distance to think about the issue). I need to think about it and we will talk later on/ tomorrow'.

And leave the space.

It's like giving yourself the opportunity to pause and restart. In this way, you don't get stuck in a specific reaction within the power struggle. You give yourself time and space to think when and how best to react in a conscious way. Then you are not only modelling self-regulation, but also re-building your authority.

Remember this is not a one-solution-fits-all situation. It's an ongoing experience of learning about you, your children and your relationship.

- 17 -
Parents as a team

The most important thing a father can do for his children is to love their mother, and the most important thing a mother can do for her children is to love their father.
Unknown source

Having parents that work collaboratively in their parenting is vital for raising healthy, confident and happy children. What follows below are a few tips and suggestions to empower you as a team, whether you are married, in partnership or divorced.

Together as one

Is this scenario familiar to you: Your partner says something to your child that you disagree with and you hold back your reaction. But then your upset child comes to you complaining or blaming your partner for the injustice that happened, and you lose it and tell your partner off in front them?

I know parents who do this all the time. They mistakenly believe this is for their children's benefit – that they are protecting them. What they don't know is that:

- Many children know exactly how to manipulate the situation to get what they want.
- Even when that's not the case, *challenging* your partner's word or decision in front of the children not only weakens their authority in the family, but it actually weakens yours as well.

Most of the time, holding your reaction and supporting your partner in front your children will give two important messages:

- The first message is for your children – that you and your partner are *one*. This makes you, as parents, stronger. It also helps your children in the long term, as they will be less anxious or stressed to be the *cause* of any conflict.

The second message is for your partners – that you trust their judgement and support them, and if anything else needs to be said you will express your disagreement and values when you are by yourselves. By doing so, you are already one step closer to working as a team. Your partner will appreciate this support and will be much more likely to consider your opinion.

The power of working together

Imagine that you are riding a two-horse carriage to get home from a long day at work. You enjoy the view, the breeze, the moment. In the middle of the journey, one horse keeps pushing forwards while the other is pulling backwards. What happens to you? You are stuck! Do you still enjoy the moment as before? No. You are probably frustrated, angry and confused, and just want to keep moving to get home.

We, the parents, are not the rider in this story. We are the horses. When we don't work together as parents, our children's emotional development can get stuck. They can't enjoy the view of their childhood because they're stuck with two horses that pull in different directions. It is a lot of emotional stress on your children when parents are locked in a power struggle.

In contrast, the power of two horses who ride in the same direction is greater than the sum of the two riding separately. The sum is greater than its parts when you work as co-parents as well.

How to navigate a dead end

To agree to disagree and to arrange another dialogue after some thinking time and create a different energy can be very beneficial. When couples disagree, unconsciously their anxiety is raised. Slowing the process down, enabling yourselves to reflect, bring different perspectives, trying to understand your partner's point of view, and keeping an open dialogue, will help to reduce that anxiety. Only then will you two be able to reach decisions that suit your family.

One step forward might be to understand that your partner loves, cares and feel responsible for your children as much as you do. They just have a different perspective on how to take care of them. What happens is that when one tries to express their view and it is not received, they become more extreme in their reaction. Slowly the couple dynamic becomes a power struggle, often something like 'good cop–bad cop', where one parent has strong boundaries and one doesn't set limits. However, when you see things from your partner's point of view, it is easier to talk about the challenges you face together rather than engage with the critical, shaming, blaming game.

In fact, you probably complement each other. One of you brings more feelings and the other more rationality. When you see such differences as a strength – bringing together two different perspectives – you are a winning team and your children will gain from it.

In the unfortunate case of repeated conflict without resolution, it is advisable to turn to a relationship counsellor or parenting advisor.

"But I'm right!"

Here's another saying for you: 'You can be right – or you can be in relationship!'.

If, because you feel you are 'right,' you dismiss, control or argue with your partner day in–day out, I can tell you that you are wrong. My mother says, 'You need to be smart – not right.' Keeping an open dialogue with your partner, especially when you disagree, creates a healthy foundation for your children and models the idea that where there are differences of opinion things can be negotiated. Telling your partners that what they're doing is wrong all the time just raises their defences. When they don't feel good about themselves, don't expect to be appreciated yourself.

Instead, try to empower each other. Listen carefully to your partner's complaints. Behind any criticism and blaming will be a clue for the change that needs to happen. Interestingly, when one partner starts to work on themselves, the whole system changes. Although you both need to change to be able to work together, you can be the first one. Start by telling your partner all the things you appreciate about the way they parent your child.

You are both right!

We recently booked a family holiday to Thailand. My husband and I had visited during our single days, so we wanted to prepare our girls for the different culture. A few weekends before the trip, I told them that '*Sawadicha'* is how you say 'hello' in Thai. My husband heard that and corrected me to '*Sawadiklap.'* I replied with 'No, no! I definitely remember *Sawadicha!*' Although my husband agreed with me that I have an excellent memory, he insisted that in this case he remembered correctly. We left it at that.

On the next weekend, while organising a training weekend for therapists, I met a therapist who is half English and half Thai. During the break, I rushed to her saying, 'You can resolve a conflict I have with my husband!' After hearing about our disagreement, she smiled and simply said, 'You are both right. If you are a woman, you say Sawadicha. If you are a man you say Sawadiklap.' How enlightening!

Although theoretically I know couples can both be right, when I feel 'right,' there is not space in my mind for this possibility. It is even more than that, because (if you're like me) when I thought I was right, the possibility of both of us being right was simply not an option! That evening, I shared the story with the family. My older daughter said, 'So you were both right!'. Yes, we were. And you, with whatever disagreement you may experience, might both be right too.

Build on couple strengths

In which area of your couple relationship do you feel that you work best as a team? Some couples work together really well around finance, others around planning family holidays, others with intimacy and sex. Whatever it is, think together what makes it work in that specific area.

- How can you bring the same spirit and quality of teamwork to your parenting style?
- What small step can you take this week that will help you parent together as a team?

Share this with your partner. Expect nothing from him or her, just share your journey and do what you need to do. As one of my mentors says 'Feel the feelings and do the right thing.' Behaviours speak louder than words.

More than one model

Remember from the Introduction to Part Two how you brought to your parenting style your 'baggage', with a specific 'model' of how to parent. Now, add to that your partner's 'baggage' and his or her 'model'. What have you got? Two systems in which you act in your own family. If the two systems are similar (let's say you both believe in healthy boundaries for children), you are less likely to experience tension around discipline. If, on the other hand, you hold two different systems – one of you believes in *authoritative* parenting and the other in a more relaxed and free style – then you are more likely to experience tension around your children. The key is to be curious. Make time for the two of you to explore these questions:

- With which model or system did you come to this relationship?
- How did each of your parents work together, or not, as parents?
- How did it feel for you as a child?
- What do you remember from conflicted events?

Then, considering both the positive and negative experiences from your childhoods, think about the 'model' you want to pass on to your children. Don't leave it with general statements – make your vision specific!

- If you were to be filmed when you and your partner are experiencing tension, would your behaviour in line with your values?
- What positive behaviour might we see in the film?
- What do you say? Do? And how do you do it?

Finally, how do you think your child will react to the positive change in the short term and the long term?

We "need" versus we "must"

The best security blanket a child can have is parents
*who respect each other—**Jane Blaustone***

I cannot stress enough how important it is to be on the same page when co-parenting. This is why I encourage parents to come together for the first session with me, so I can hear both of their valuable and equal perspectives. It also provides the opportunity to start the change process *on the same page*. When you let issues with children divide you, everyone loses – you, your partner, but mostly your children. Try to see things from your child's perspective. Think about the last time there was tension between you and your partner in front of your child.

- What did your child understand from your body language, from your attitude and the way you handled the conflict?
- What would you like them to experience in such moments?
- How can you express yourself in a way that will achieve that?

We may say to ourselves 'We *need* to work together – we will try' but if you aren't happy with what your child experiences when you and your partner disagree, this is *not* enough. When we say 'We *must* work together' we will find a way to achieve that. No other option here.

Reading the right team-sheet

Some parents start to explain a challenge in their co-parenting by saying 'We … and they …'. I have learned to ask 'Who is *we*?' Very often the *we* stands for the parent I'm talking with, and the child, whereas the *they* stands for the other parent. There is a sense of 'us' versus 'them'.

In other cases, I hear about parents who want to be their children's best friends. Your child can and should make their own friends. They don't need you as friends. They need you as parents: parents who reach decisions together; parents who work as a team – a team that knows how to work through differences with respect and love. And if the disagreement is about a sensitive issue, or loaded with emotional baggage, then keep it behind closed doors.

Never use your children in a conflict, especially by blaming, criticising or shaming the other parent. You and your partner are on the same team with the same goals. It's important for your children to experience that. Your children cannot feel loved if they are in the middle of parental tension, and very often they will try to find ways to take advantage of the split between you.

129

Keep cultivating the couple

Harville Handrix and Helen LaKelly-Hunt devoted their lives to finding out why couples fight and what couples want from their relationships. They found that couples want three fundamental qualities and indicators of a successful intimate relationship:

- The first is safety. Knowing that being with their partner, or having their partner supporting them, makes them feel safe.
- The second which builds on safety – the sense of connection.
- The third is the feeling of joyful aliveness when they are together. In other words, they have fun together.

Do you remember the days before you became parents? Did it feel like a safer, more connected and joyful relationship? You have the power to bring it back! Ask yourself:

- Are you a partner who provides safety?
- Are you a partner who provides moments and opportunities for connection?
- Are you creating times of high-energy fun together?

If you think that this has nothing to do with parenting issues, think again!

It all starts with you as a *couple*. To be the best parent you can be you *have* to be a best partner you can be. Bring the fun back to your relationship, so your children can see there is a reason to grow up; that relationships matter and are worth investing in.

Adults, beside mortgages, work, and endless tasks, can and must have space for fun and playfulness. Magically, when you have more fun in your relationship, some of the problems with your children simply fade away.

Putting it all together

When a challenge in the relationship you have with your children occurs, it's important to see the Big Picture. Treating 'the problem' in isolation, without addressing the whole dynamic in the family, will lead to little improvement.

Furthermore, many of the issues parents present in my clinic are behaviours that they themselves, consciously or unconsciously, implanted in their children.

So creating a real and stable change requires self-reflection, awareness, energy and new skills and understanding to recognise that challenge represents a growth opportunity for your children, you and your relationship.

Your children look at you, but they don't see only you. In your eyes, they see their own reflection as well. They see what you see in them and what you think about them. By looking at you, they also have a sense of their capacity to cope with a challenge, and their strengths and weaknesses, and your belief in them.

They also look at you and learn what is important in life. How you are with your partner, parents, siblings and friends. How you are as a person. They are scanning your 'way of being'.

- Do you have your own goals in life or is all your happiness on their shoulders?
- Are you appreciating small things in life, or inclined to complain about things?
- Are you taking responsibility or being the 'victim' of situations and people?
- Are you creating your own moments of happiness or depending on the happiness of others?
- Do you learn from and forgive yourself for mistakes or treat yourself harshly with guilt and shame?

They're making notes. *Be the person you want them to be* when they grow up.

With the conflicting advice they get, today's parents risk losing touch with what is important. It's not the overbooked activities or academic pressure that will make your child a better person.

It's not the stickers, screen time or time-outs that will teach them your key values. It's through encouragement, having healthy boundaries, good modelling, belief in your children, placing appropriate responsibilities on their shoulders and letting them experience a positive, stable and consistent, reliable connection with you, that will make the difference.

Your actions today, as a parent and a partner, shape the person they will be tomorrow and in the years to come. You want them to show their best selves. So show your best self now and use the challenge you are facing as an opportunity for growth and healing.

Who knows, in the years to come you might, as Freud said, look back and remember this time as the most beautiful one of all.

Sources and resources

Ben-Ari K. *The Feelings Cake*. Available at: https://www.youtube.com/watch?v=ZK99JsyHhLQ.

Bor W, Sanders MR and Markie-Dadds C. The effects of the Triple-P Positive Parenting Program on preschool children with co-occurring disruptive behaviour and attentional/hyperactive difficulties. *Journal of Abnormal Child Psychology* 2002, 30(6), 571–87.

Dimberg U, Thunberg M and Elmehed K. Unconscious facial reactions to emotional facial expressions. *Psychological Science* 2000, 11(1), 86–89.

Dweck C. *Mindset - Updated Edition: Changing The Way You Think To Fulfil Your Potential*. 2017, Rubinson.

Faber A and Mazlish E. *How To Talk So Children Will Listen*. 2012, Piccadilly Press.

Graham AM, Fisher P and Pfeifer J. What sleeping babies hear: A functional MRI study of interparental conflict and infants. *Psychological Science* 2013, 24(5), 782–89.

Haim G. *Between a Parent and a Child*. 2004, Crown Publications.

Hendrix H and LaKelly Hunt H. *Connected Parent, Thriving Children*. Available at: http://imagorelationships.org/pub/find-a-workshop/connected-parents-thriving-kids-programs/.

Hendrix H and LaKelly Hunt H. *Giving The Love That Heals*, 1998, Simon & Schuster.

Jung C. *Integration of the Personality*. 1946, Kegan Paul, Trench, Trubner & Co.

Leboyer F. *Loving Hands: The Traditional Indian Art of Baby Massage*. 1997, Newmarket Press.

Levesque RJR (Ed.) *Encyclopedia of Adolescence*, 2011, Springer.

Love P and Stosny S. *How to Improve Your Marriage Without Talking About It*. 2008, Broadway Books.

Manning M and Granstrom B. *How Did I Begin?* 2004, Franklin Watts.

Provire R. Contagious laughter: Laughter is a sufficient stimulus for laughs and smiles. *Bulletin of the Psychonomic Society* 1992, 30(1), 1–4.

Redding RE, Mulford C and Mendoza MM. *Training for Effective Parenting*. In: RJR Levesque (Ed.) *Encyclopedia of Adolescence*. Springer.

Siegel DJ and Harzell M. *Parenting from The Inside Out*. 2014, Scribe.

Index

Printed in Great Britain
by Amazon